Italian Cookbook:

Unlock the Secrets to Authentic Italian Cuisine with 150 Delicious Recipes

Disclaimer

While every effort has been made to ensure the accuracy of the information in this cookbook, the author and publisher accept no responsibility for errors or omissions, or for any consequences arising from the use of the information contained herein.

This cookbook is intended to provide general information on the topics presented and is not an exhaustive treatment of such subjects. All recipes are intended to be prepared by adults or with adult supervision and the author and publisher are not responsible for any injuries or damages that may result.

The reader assumes all risks associated with the preparation and consumption of the dishes detailed in this cookbook. Always consult a medical professional before making significant changes to your diet.

Table of Contents

Breakfast

Cornetto (Italian Croissant)
Yield: 6 servings | Prep time: 20 minutes | Cook time: 15 minutes

Ingredients:

- 2 cups all-purpose flour
- 1/4 cup granulated sugar
- 1 tsp active dry yeast
- 1/2 tsp salt
- Powdered sugar, for dusting
- 1/2 cup cold unsalted butter, cubed
- 1/2 cup lukewarm milk
- 1 tsp vanilla extract
- 1 beaten egg

Directions:

1. Combine flour, sugar, yeast, and salt. Cut in cold butter.
2. Mix lukewarm milk and vanilla extract. Add to flour mixture and stir to form a dough.
3. Knead dough for 5 minutes, then let it rise for 1 hour.
4. Preheat oven to 400°F (200°C). Line a baking sheet with parchment paper.
5. Divide dough into 6 portions. Roll each into a triangle, then roll up into croissant shape.
6. Place croissants on the baking sheet. Brush with beaten egg.
7. Bake for 12-15 minutes until golden brown.
8. Cool on a wire rack and dust with powdered sugar.

Nutritional Information: (per serving) Calories: 310 Protein: 5g Carbohydrates: 35g Fat: 17g Fiber: 1g Cholesterol: 70mg Sodium: 190mg Potassium: 100mg

Caffè Latte (Coffee with Milk)
Yield: 2 servings | Prep time: 5 minutes | Cook time: 5 minutes

Ingredients:

- 2 cups brewed coffee
- Sugar or sweetener (optional)
- 1 cup milk

Directions:

1. Brew 2 cups of coffee.
2. Heat milk in a saucepan or microwave until hot.
3. Froth the milk using a frother or by whisking vigorously.
4. Divide the coffee between two cups.
5. Pour the frothed milk over the coffee.
6. Add sugar or sweetener, if desired.
7. Stir gently to combine.
8. Serve and enjoy your Caffè Latte!

Nutritional Information: (per serving) Calories: 40 Protein: 2g Carbohydrates: 6g Fat: 1g Fiber: 0g Cholesterol: 5mg Sodium: 40mg Potassium: 120mg

Pane e Nutella (Bread with Nutella)
Yield: 2 servings | Prep time: 5 minutes | Cook time: N/A (No cooking required)

Ingredients:

- 4 slices of bread (such as white bread or brioche)
- Nutella (as needed)

Directions:

1. Take 4 slices of bread.
2. Spread Nutella generously on one side of each bread slice.
3. Sandwich the bread slices together, Nutella side facing inwards.
4. Cut the sandwich in half diagonally or into desired shapes.
5. Serve immediately and enjoy your delicious Pane e Nutella!

Nutritional Information: (per serving) Calories: 300 Protein: 6g Carbohydrates: 40g Fat: 14g Fiber: 2g Cholesterol: 0mg Sodium: 200mg Potassium: 100mg

Bomboloni (Italian Donuts)
Yield: 6 servings | Prep time: 20 minutes | Cook time: 10 minutes

Ingredients:

- 2 cups all-purpose flour
- 1/4 cup granulated sugar
- 1 packet (2 1/4 tsp) active dry yeast
- 1/2 tsp salt
- Powdered sugar, for dusting
- 1/2 cup whole milk
- 2 large eggs
- 2 tbsp softened unsalted butter
- Vegetable oil, for frying

Directions:

1. Mix flour, sugar, yeast, and salt in a bowl.
2. Warm milk and add it to the dry ingredients with eggs and softened butter. Mix into a sticky dough.
3. Knead the dough for 5 minutes, then let it rise for 1 hour.
4. Roll out the dough and cut circles.
5. Let the circles rise for 30 minutes.
6. Heat vegetable oil to 350°F (175°C) in a saucepan or fryer.
7. Fry the dough circles for 2-3 minutes on each side until golden brown.
8. Drain the fried bomboloni on paper towels.
9. Dust with powdered sugar before serving.

Nutritional Information: (per serving) Calories: 260 Protein: 6g Carbohydrates: 42g Fat: 7g Fiber: 1g Cholesterol: 65mg Sodium: 100mg Potassium: 90mg

Frittata (Italian Omelette)

Yield: 4 servings | Prep time: 10 minutes | Cook time: 15 minutes

Ingredients:

- 6 large eggs
- 1/4 cup milk
- Salt and pepper
- 1 tbsp olive oil
- Fresh herbs (optional)
- 1/2 onion, chopped
- 1/2 bell pepper, diced
- 1 cup diced cooked ham or vegetables
- 1/2 cup shredded cheese

Directions:

1. Whisk eggs, milk, salt, and pepper in a bowl.
2. Heat olive oil in a skillet and cook onion and bell pepper until softened.
3. Add ham or vegetables and cook for 2 minutes.
4. Pour the egg mixture into the skillet, covering the ingredients evenly.
5. Sprinkle shredded cheese on top.
6. Cook on the stove for 5-7 minutes until the edges set.
7. Broil in the oven for 2-3 minutes until golden and set.
8. Let it cool slightly before slicing.
9. Garnish with fresh herbs, if desired.
10. Serve warm or at room temperature.

Nutritional Information: (per serving) Calories: 230 Protein: 16g Carbohydrates: 5g Fat: 16g Fiber: 1g Cholesterol: 370mg Sodium: 430mg Potassium: 240mg

Prosciutto e Melone (Prosciutto and Melon)

Yield: 4 servings | Prep time: 10 minutes | Cook time: N/A (No cooking required)

Ingredients:

- 1 ripe cantaloupe melon
- 8 slices of prosciutto

Directions:

1. Cut the cantaloupe melon in half and remove the seeds.
2. Use a melon baller or a spoon to scoop out small balls of melon flesh.
3. Arrange the prosciutto slices on a serving platter or individual plates.
4. Place a melon ball on each slice of prosciutto.
5. Serve immediately and enjoy the delightful combination of sweet melon and savory prosciutto.

Nutritional Information: (per serving) Calories: 150 Protein: 8g Carbohydrates: 15g Fat: 6g Fiber: 2g Cholesterol: 20mg Sodium: 850mg Potassium: 500mg

Brioche con Gelato (Brioche with Gelato)
Yield: 4 servings | Prep time: 15 minutes | Cook time: 10 minutes

Ingredients:

- 4 brioche buns
- 4 scoops of your favorite gelato flavors
- Powdered sugar, for dusting (optional)
- 1 tablespoon unsalted butter, melted

Directions:

1. Preheat the oven to 350°F (175°C).
2. Slice the brioche buns in half horizontally, creating a top and bottom piece.
3. Brush the insides of the buns with melted butter.
4. Place the buns on a baking sheet and toast them in the oven for about 5 minutes, until lightly golden.
5. Remove the buns from the oven and let them cool for a few minutes.
6. Place a scoop of gelato onto the bottom half of each brioche bun.
7. Gently press the top half of the bun onto the gelato, creating a sandwich.
8. Dust the tops of the brioche buns with powdered sugar, if desired.
9. Serve immediately and enjoy!

Nutritional Information (per serving): Calories: 350 Protein: 6g Carbohydrates: 52g Fat: 14g Fiber: 1g Cholesterol: 60mg Sodium: 200mg Potassium: 180mg

Ciambella (Italian Ring-Shaped Cake)
Yield: 8 servings | Prep time: 15 minutes | Cook time: 40 minutes

Ingredients:

- 2 cups all-purpose flour
- 1 1/2 tsp baking powder
- 1/4 tsp salt
- 1/2 cup unsalted butter, softened
- 1 cup granulated sugar
- Powdered sugar, for dusting
- 3 large eggs
- 1 tsp vanilla extract
- 1/2 cup milk
- Zest of 1 lemon

Directions:

1. Preheat oven to 350°F (175°C). Grease and flour a ciambella or bundt pan.
2. Whisk flour, baking powder, and salt together in a bowl.
3. Cream butter and sugar in a large bowl until light and fluffy.
4. Beat in eggs one at a time, followed by vanilla extract.
5. Gradually add dry ingredients and milk to the wet mixture, alternating between them. Mix until just combined. Stir in lemon zest. Pour batter into prepared pan and smooth the top.
6. Bake for 35-40 minutes or until a toothpick inserted into the center comes out clean.
7. Cool in the pan for 10 minutes, then transfer to a wire rack to cool completely.
8. Dust with powdered sugar before serving.

Nutritional Information (per serving): Calories: 280 Protein: 4g Carbohydrates: 42g Fat: 11g Fiber: 1g Cholesterol: 75mg Sodium: 120mg Potassium: 80mg

Yogurt con Frutta (Yogurt with Fruit)
Yield: 4 servings | Prep time: 10 minutes | Cook time: 0 minutes

Ingredients:

- 2 cups plain yogurt
- 1 cup mixed fresh fruits (such as berries, sliced bananas, diced mangoes)
- 1/4 cup granola or nuts (optional for topping)
- 2 tablespoons honey or maple syrup

Directions:

1. In a serving bowl, spoon the plain yogurt.
2. Arrange the mixed fresh fruits on top of the yogurt.
3. Drizzle honey or maple syrup over the fruit and yogurt.
4. If desired, sprinkle granola or nuts on top for added crunch.
5. Gently mix the yogurt, fruit, and sweetener together to combine.
6. Serve immediately and enjoy this refreshing and nutritious yogurt with fruit!

Nutritional Information (per serving): Calories: 180 Protein: 8g Carbohydrates: 32g Fat: 3g Fiber: 2g Cholesterol: 10mg Sodium: 80mg Potassium: 320mg

Panettone (Italian Sweet Bread)
Yield: 1 panettone | Prep time: 30 minutes | Cook time: 40 minutes

Ingredients:

- 3 1/2 cups all-purpose flour
- 1/2 cup granulated sugar
- 1/2 tsp salt
- 1/2 cup unsalted butter, softened
- 4 large eggs
- 2 tsp active dry yeast
- Powdered sugar, for dusting
- 1/2 cup lukewarm milk
- 1/2 cup mixed candied fruits
- 1/4 cup raisins
- Zest of 1 lemon
- Zest of 1 orange
- 1 tsp vanilla extract

Directions:

1. Combine flour, sugar, and salt in a bowl.
2. Dissolve yeast in lukewarm milk and let it sit for 5 minutes until frothy.
3. Add butter, eggs, candied fruits, raisins, lemon zest, orange zest, and vanilla extract to the flour mixture.
4. Pour in the yeast-milk mixture and mix until sticky dough forms.
5. Knead the dough on a floured surface for 10 minutes until smooth.
6. Let the dough rise in a greased bowl for 2 hours until doubled in size. Preheat the oven to 350°F (175°C).
7. Shape the dough into a round loaf and place it on a lined baking sheet.
8. Let the loaf rise for 1 hour. Bake for 40-45 minutes until golden and a toothpick comes out clean.
9. Cool the panettone on a wire rack.
10. Dust with powdered sugar before serving.

Nutritional Information (per serving): Calories: 290 Protein: 6g Carbohydrates: 52g Fat: 7g Fiber: 2g Cholesterol: 65mg Sodium: 80mg Potassium: 140mg

Tiramisù Pancakes

Yield: 4 servings | Prep time: 15 minutes | Cook time: 15 minutes

Ingredients:

- 1 cup all-purpose flour
- 2 tbsp granulated sugar
- 1 1/2 tsp baking powder
- 1/4 tsp salt
- 1 cup milk
- 1 large egg
- Ladyfinger cookies, for serving (optional)

- 1 tsp vanilla extract
- 2 tbsp instant coffee powder
- 2 tbsp hot water
- 1 cup mascarpone cheese
- 2 tbsp powdered sugar
- Cocoa powder, for dusting

Directions:

1. Whisk flour, sugar, baking powder, and salt in a bowl.
2. Combine milk, egg, and vanilla extract in a separate bowl. Add to dry ingredients and mix.
3. Dissolve instant coffee in hot water.
4. Whisk mascarpone cheese and powdered sugar until creamy.
5. Heat a greased skillet over medium heat. Pour 1/4 cup of batter for each pancake. Cook until golden.
6. Spread mascarpone mixture on each pancake. Drizzle with coffee mixture.
7. Stack the pancakes, dust with cocoa powder.
8. Serve with ladyfinger cookies on the side, if desired.

Nutritional Information (per serving): Calories: 320 Protein: 8g Carbohydrates: 40g Fat: 14g Fiber: 1g Cholesterol: 70mg Sodium: 230mg Potassium: 180mg

Crostata di Marmellata (Italian Jam Tart)

Yield: 6 servings | Prep time: 20 minutes | Cook time: 25 minutes

Ingredients:

- 2 cups all-purpose flour
- 1/2 cup granulated sugar
- 1/4 tsp salt
- 1/2 cup unsalted butter, cold and diced
- Powdered sugar, for dusting

- 1 large egg
- 1/2 tsp vanilla extract
- 1/2 cup jam (your choice of flavor)

Directions:

1. Mix flour, sugar, and salt.
2. Cut cold diced butter into the flour mixture until it resembles coarse crumbs.
3. Beat egg and vanilla extract together, then add to the flour mixture.
4. Form the dough, refrigerate for 30 minutes. Roll out the dough and fit into a 9-inch tart pan.
5. Spread jam over the dough. Bake at 375°F (190°C) for 25 minutes until golden.
6. Cool the tart completely.
7. Dust with powdered sugar before serving.

Nutritional Information (per serving): Calories: 330 Protein: 4g Carbohydrates: 53g Fat: 11g Fiber: 1g Cholesterol: 60mg Sodium: 75mg Potassium: 55mg

Cappuccino e Cornetto (Cappuccino and Croissant)
Yield: 2 servings | Prep time: 5 minutes | Cook time: 10 minutes

Ingredients:

- 2 cups milk
- 2 shots of espresso or 1/2 cup strong brewed coffee
- Cocoa powder, for dusting
- 2 tbsp granulated sugar
- 2 croissants

Directions:

1. Heat milk in a saucepan until hot but not boiling. Brew espresso or strong coffee.
2. Froth the hot milk until creamy and frothy.
3. Pour brewed espresso or coffee into two cups.
4. Add 1 tbsp of sugar to each cup and stir until dissolved.
5. Pour frothed milk into cups, dividing it evenly.
6. Stir gently to combine coffee and milk.
7. Warm croissants in the oven.
8. Serve cappuccino with warm croissants.
9. Dust cappuccino with cocoa powder.

Nutritional Information (per serving): Calories: 300 Protein: 10g Carbohydrates: 40g Fat: 10g Fiber: 2g Cholesterol: 25mg Sodium: 150mg Potassium: 400mg

Torta della Nonna (Grandma's Cake)
Yield: 6 servings | Prep time: 20 minutes | Cook time: 40 minutes

Ingredients:

- 2 sheets of ready-made puff pastry
- 2 cups milk
- 4 egg yolks
- 1/2 cup granulated sugar
- Powdered sugar, for dusting
- 1/4 cup all-purpose flour
- 1/2 tsp vanilla extract
- Zest of 1 lemon
- 1/4 cup pine nuts

Directions:

1. Line a greased round cake pan with one sheet of puff pastry.
2. Heat milk in a saucepan until steaming.
3. Whisk together egg yolks, sugar, flour, vanilla extract, and lemon zest.
4. Slowly pour steaming milk into the egg mixture, whisking continuously.
5. Cook custard mixture until thickened, stirring constantly.
6. Pour custard over the puff pastry in the cake pan.
7. Sprinkle pine nuts evenly over the custard.
8. Cover with the second sheet of puff pastry and seal the edges.
9. Bake at 350°F (180°C) for about 40 minutes until golden brown.
10. Let the cake cool completely.
11. Dust with powdered sugar before serving.

Nutritional Information (per serving): Calories: 380 Protein: 6g Carbohydrates: 48g Fat: 18g Fiber: 1g Cholesterol: 115mg Sodium: 100mg Potassium: 180mg

Crema di Mascarpone e Frutti di Bosco (Mascarpone Cream with Berries)

Yield: 4 servings | Prep time: 10 minutes | Cook time: 15 minutes

Ingredients:

- 8 oz mascarpone cheese
- 1/4 cup powdered sugar
- 1 tsp vanilla extract
- Mint leaves, for garnish (optional)

- 1 cup mixed berries (such as strawberries, blueberries, raspberries)

Directions:

1. In a mixing bowl, combine mascarpone cheese, powdered sugar, and vanilla extract.
2. Whip the mixture until smooth and creamy.
3. Wash and dry the mixed berries.
4. Divide the mascarpone cream into serving dishes or glasses.
5. Top with the mixed berries.
6. Garnish with mint leaves, if desired.
7. Serve immediately and enjoy!

Nutritional Information (per serving): Calories: 280 Protein: 6g Carbohydrates: 15g Fat: 21g Fiber: 2g Cholesterol: 70mg Sodium: 30mg Potassium: 150mg

Italian Salads dishes

Caprese Salad
Yield: 4 servings | Prep time: 10 minutes | Cook time: 15 minutes

Ingredients:

- 4 ripe tomatoes
- 8 oz fresh mozzarella cheese
- Handful of fresh basil leaves
- Salt and pepper, to taste
- Extra-virgin olive oil
- Balsamic vinegar

Directions:

1. Slice the tomatoes and fresh mozzarella cheese into 1/4-inch thick slices.
2. Arrange the tomato and mozzarella slices on a serving platter, alternating them.
3. Tuck fresh basil leaves between the tomato and mozzarella slices.
4. Drizzle the salad with extra-virgin olive oil and balsamic vinegar.
5. Season with salt and pepper to taste.
6. Let the flavors meld for a few minutes before serving.
7. Enjoy the Caprese Salad as a refreshing and light appetizer or side dish.

Nutritional Information (per serving): Calories: 220 Protein: 14g Carbohydrates: 6g Fat: 16g Fiber: 2g Cholesterol: 35mg Sodium: 320mg Potassium: 380mg

Panzanella Salad
Yield: 4 servings | Prep time: 15 minutes | Cook time: 20 minutes

Ingredients:

- 4 cups stale bread, preferably rustic Italian bread, cubed
- 2 large tomatoes, diced
- 1 cucumber, diced
- Salt and pepper, to taste
- 1 red onion, thinly sliced
- 1/2 cup fresh basil leaves, torn
- 1/4 cup extra-virgin olive oil
- 2 tablespoons red wine vinegar

Directions:

1. In a large bowl, combine the bread cubes, tomatoes, cucumber, red onion, and basil leaves.
2. Drizzle the olive oil and red wine vinegar over the ingredients.
3. Season with salt and pepper to taste.
4. Toss the salad gently to ensure the bread soaks up the dressing and flavors.
5. Let the Panzanella Salad sit for 10 minutes to allow the bread to soften slightly.
6. Serve the salad at room temperature, allowing the flavors to meld together.
7. Enjoy this refreshing and hearty Italian bread salad as a main dish or side.

Nutritional Information (per serving): Calories: 270 Protein: 5g Carbohydrates: 30g Fat: 15g Fiber: 3g Cholesterol: 0mg Sodium: 320mg Potassium: 380mg

Insalata di Rucola e Parmigiano (Arugula and Parmesan Salad)

Yield: 4 servings | Prep time: 10 minutes | Cook time: 15 minutes

Ingredients:

- 4 cups fresh arugula leaves
- 1/2 cup shaved Parmesan cheese
- Salt and pepper, to taste
- 1/4 cup extra-virgin olive oil
- 2 tablespoons lemon juice

Directions:

1. In a large salad bowl, add the fresh arugula leaves.
2. Sprinkle the shaved Parmesan cheese over the arugula.
3. Drizzle the extra-virgin olive oil and lemon juice over the salad.
4. Season with salt and pepper to taste.
5. Toss the salad gently to coat the arugula leaves evenly with the dressing.
6. Adjust the seasoning if needed.
7. Serve the Arugula and Parmesan Salad as a refreshing side dish or starter.

Nutritional Information (per serving): Calories: 160 Protein: 6g Carbohydrates: 3g Fat: 14g Fiber: 1g Cholesterol: 5mg Sodium: 180mg Potassium: 200mg

Insalata di Mare (Seafood Salad)

Yield: 4 servings | Prep time: 20 minutes | Cook time: 10 minutes

Ingredients:

- 1 pound mixed seafood (such as shrimp, calamari, and mussels), cooked and cooled
- 1/2 cup cherry tomatoes, halved
- 1/4 cup red onion, thinly sliced
- Salt and pepper, to taste
- 1/4 cup fresh parsley, chopped
- 2 tablespoons capers
- 2 tablespoons extra-virgin olive oil
- 1 tablespoon lemon juice

Directions:

1. In a large bowl, combine the cooked seafood, cherry tomatoes, red onion, parsley, and capers.
2. In a separate small bowl, whisk together the extra-virgin olive oil and lemon juice to make the dressing.
3. Pour the dressing over the seafood mixture.
4. Season with salt and pepper to taste..
5. Gently toss all the ingredients together to coat them with the dressing.
6. Allow the Insalata di Mare to marinate in the refrigerator for at least 10 minutes before serving.
7. Serve the salad chilled as a delicious appetizer or main course.

Nutritional Information (per serving): Calories: 240 Protein: 25g Carbohydrates: 5g Fat: 14g Fiber: 1g Cholesterol: 180mg Sodium: 420mg Potassium: 400mg

Insalata di Pollo (Chicken Salad)

Yield: 4 servings | Prep time: 15 minutes | Cook time: 20 minutes

Ingredients:

- 2 boneless, skinless chicken breasts
- 4 cups mixed salad greens
- 1 cup cherry tomatoes, halved
- 1/2 cucumber, sliced
- 1/4 red onion, thinly sliced
- Salt and pepper, to taste

- 1/4 cup Kalamata olives, pitted
- 2 tablespoons fresh basil, chopped
- 2 tablespoons extra-virgin olive oil
- 1 tablespoon balsamic vinegar

Directions:

1. Season the chicken breasts with salt and pepper. Grill or bake them until cooked through, about 15-20 minutes. Let them cool, then slice into strips.
2. In a large salad bowl, combine the mixed salad greens, cherry tomatoes, cucumber, red onion, Kalamata olives, and fresh basil.
3. In a small bowl, whisk together the extra-virgin olive oil and balsamic vinegar to make the dressing.
4. Add the sliced chicken to the salad bowl. Drizzle the dressing over the salad and chicken.
5. Toss all the ingredients together to coat them with the dressing.
6. Adjust the seasoning with salt and pepper, if needed.
7. Serve the Insalata di Pollo as a satisfying and flavorful main course.

Nutritional Information (per serving): Calories: 280 Protein: 28g Carbohydrates: 8g Fat: 16g Fiber: 3g Cholesterol: 75mg Sodium: 400mg Potassium: 560mg

Insalata di Tonno (Tuna Salad)

Yield: 4 servings | Prep time: 10 minutes | Cook time: 0 minutes

Ingredients:

- 2 cans (5 ounces each) tuna, drained
- 4 cups mixed salad greens
- 1/2 red bell pepper, diced
- 1/2 cucumber, diced
- 1/4 red onion, thinly sliced
- Salt and pepper, to taste

- 1/4 cup Kalamata olives, pitted
- 2 tablespoons capers
- 2 tablespoons fresh parsley, chopped
- 2 tablespoons lemon juice
- 2 tablespoons extra-virgin olive oil

Directions:

1. In a large salad bowl, combine the mixed salad greens, diced red bell pepper, cucumber, red onion, Kalamata olives, capers, and fresh parsley.
2. Flake the drained tuna into the bowl, distributing it evenly.
3. In a small bowl, whisk together the lemon juice, extra-virgin olive oil, salt, and pepper to make the dressing. Pour the dressing over the salad and tuna. Toss all the ingredients together gently to coat them with the dressing. Adjust the seasoning with salt and pepper, if needed.
4. Serve the Insalata di Tonno as a light and refreshing meal.

Nutritional Information (per serving): Calories: 220 Protein: 24g Carbohydrates: 7g Fat: 11g Fiber: 2g Cholesterol: 30mg Sodium: 520mg Potassium: 390mg

Insalata di Gamberi (Shrimp Salad)

Yield: 4 servings | Prep time: 15 minutes | Cook time: 5 minutes

Ingredients:

- 1 pound shrimp, peeled and deveined
- 4 cups mixed salad greens
- 1 cup cherry tomatoes, halved
- 1/2 cucumber, diced
- 1/4 red onion, thinly sliced
- Salt and pepper, to taste
- 1/4 cup fresh basil leaves, torn
- 2 tablespoons lemon juice
- 2 tablespoons extra-virgin olive oil
- 1 clove garlic, minced

Directions:

1. In a large pot of salted boiling water, cook the shrimp for 2-3 minutes until they turn pink and opaque. Drain and set aside.
2. In a salad bowl, combine the mixed salad greens, cherry tomatoes, diced cucumber, red onion, and torn basil leaves.
3. In a small bowl, whisk together the lemon juice, extra-virgin olive oil, minced garlic, salt, and pepper to make the dressing. Add the cooked shrimp to the salad bowl.
4. Pour the dressing over the salad and shrimp.
5. Toss all the ingredients together gently to coat them with the dressing.
6. Adjust the seasoning with salt and pepper, if needed.
7. Serve the Insalata di Gamberi as a refreshing and satisfying meal.

Nutritional Information (per serving): Calories: 180 Protein: 23g Carbohydrates: 6g Fat: 7g Fiber: 2g Cholesterol: 220mg Sodium: 380mg Potassium: 320mg

Insalata di Carciofi (Artichoke Salad)

Yield: 4 servings | Prep time: 15 minutes | Cook time: 10 minutes

Ingredients:

- 2 cans (14 ounces each) artichoke hearts, drained and quartered
- 2 cups arugula
- 1 cup cherry tomatoes, halved
- 1/4 cup red onion, thinly sliced
- Fresh basil leaves, for garnish (optional)
- 1/4 cup Kalamata olives, pitted and halved
- 2 tablespoons fresh lemon juice
- 2 tablespoons extra-virgin olive oil
- 1 clove garlic, minced
- Salt and pepper, to taste

Directions:

1. In a large bowl, combine the artichoke hearts, arugula, cherry tomatoes, red onion, and Kalamata olives.
2. In a small bowl, whisk together the lemon juice, extra-virgin olive oil, minced garlic, salt, and pepper to make the dressing. Pour the dressing over the salad ingredients and toss gently to coat.
3. Let the salad marinate for about 10 minutes to allow the flavors to meld together.
4. Garnish with fresh basil leaves, if desired.
5. Serve the Insalata di Carciofi as a refreshing and flavorful side dish or light lunch.

Nutritional Information (per serving): Calories: 150 Protein: 3g Carbohydrates: 12g Fat: 10g Fiber: 5g Cholesterol: 0mg Sodium: 500mg Potassium: 300mg

Insalata di Fagioli (Bean Salad)

Yield: 4 servings | Prep time: 10 minutes | Cook time: 0 minutes

Ingredients:

- 2 cans (15 ounces each) mixed beans, rinsed and drained
- 1/2 red bell pepper, diced
- 1/2 yellow bell pepper, diced
- 1/2 small red onion, finely chopped
- Salt and pepper, to taste
- 1/4 cup fresh parsley, chopped
- 2 tablespoons extra-virgin olive oil
- 2 tablespoons red wine vinegar
- 1 clove garlic, minced

Directions:

1. In a large bowl, combine the mixed beans, diced red and yellow bell peppers, chopped red onion, and fresh parsley.
2. In a small bowl, whisk together the extra-virgin olive oil, red wine vinegar, minced garlic, salt, and pepper to make the dressing.
3. Pour the dressing over the bean mixture and toss gently to coat.
4. Let the salad sit for a few minutes to allow the flavors to meld together.
5. Adjust the seasoning if needed.
6. Serve the Insalata di Fagioli as a healthy and nutritious side dish or light lunch option.

Nutritional Information (per serving): Calories: 220 Protein: 10g Carbohydrates: 33g Fat: 6g Fiber: 11g Cholesterol: 0mg Sodium: 400mg Potassium: 700mg

Insalata di Pomodori (Tomato Salad)

Yield: 4 servings | Prep time: 10 minutes | Cook time: 0 minutes

Ingredients:

- 4 large tomatoes, ripe and juicy
- 1/4 red onion, thinly sliced
- 1/4 cup fresh basil leaves, torn
- Salt and pepper, to taste
- 2 tablespoons extra-virgin olive oil
- 1 tablespoon balsamic vinegar

Directions:

1. Slice the tomatoes into thick slices and arrange them on a serving platter.
2. Scatter the thinly sliced red onion and torn basil leaves over the tomatoes.
3. Drizzle the extra-virgin olive oil and balsamic vinegar over the salad.
4. Season with salt and pepper to taste.
5. Let the salad sit for a few minutes to allow the flavors to meld together.
6. Serve the Insalata di Pomodori as a refreshing side dish or appetizer.

Nutritional Information (per serving): Calories: 80 Protein: 2g Carbohydrates: 7g Fat: 6g Fiber: 2g Cholesterol: 0mg Sodium: 10mg Potassium: 350mg

Insalata di Cetrioli (Cucumber Salad)

Yield: 4 servings | Prep time: 10 minutes | Cook time: 0 minutes

Ingredients:

- 2 large cucumbers
- 1/4 red onion, thinly sliced
- 2 tablespoons fresh dill, chopped
- Salt and pepper, to taste
- 2 tablespoons white wine vinegar
- 1 tablespoon extra-virgin olive oil

Directions:

1. Peel the cucumbers and slice them thinly.
2. Place the sliced cucumbers in a bowl and add the thinly sliced red onion and chopped dill.
3. Drizzle the white wine vinegar and extra-virgin olive oil over the cucumber mixture.
4. Season with salt and pepper to taste.
5. Toss everything together until well combined.
6. Let the salad marinate in the refrigerator for at least 30 minutes to allow the flavors to meld together.
7. Serve the Insalata di Cetrioli chilled as a refreshing side dish.

Nutritional Information (per serving): Calories: 35 Protein: 1g Carbohydrates: 5g Fat: 2g Fiber: 1g Cholesterol: 0mg Sodium: 5mg Potassium: 250mg

Insalata di Finocchio (Fennel Salad)

Yield: 4 servings | Prep time: 15 minutes | Cook time: 0 minutes

Ingredients:

- 2 large fennel bulbs
- 1/2 lemon
- 2 tablespoons extra-virgin olive oil
- Fresh parsley leaves, for garnish
- 1/2 teaspoon salt
- 1/4 teaspoon black pepper

Directions:

1. Trim the stalks and fronds from the fennel bulbs. Reserve a few fronds for garnish.
2. Cut the fennel bulbs in half lengthwise, then thinly slice them crosswise.
3. Squeeze the juice of half a lemon over the sliced fennel to prevent discoloration.
4. In a separate bowl, whisk together the extra-virgin olive oil, salt, and black pepper.
5. Add the sliced fennel to the dressing and toss until well coated.
6. Let the salad marinate for about 10 minutes to allow the flavors to meld together.
7. Garnish with reserved fennel fronds and fresh parsley leaves.
8. Serve the Insalata di Finocchio as a refreshing side salad.

Nutritional Information (per serving): Calories: 70 Protein: 1g Carbohydrates: 6g Fat: 5g Fiber: 3g Cholesterol: 0mg Sodium: 300mg Potassium: 360mg

Insalata di Patate (Potato Salad)

Yield: 4 servings | Prep time: 15 minutes | Cook time: 20 minutes

Ingredients:

- 1.5 pounds (680g) potatoes
- 1/4 cup mayonnaise
- 2 tablespoons Dijon mustard
- 1 tablespoon white wine vinegar
- 2 tablespoons chopped fresh parsley
- 1/2 teaspoon salt
- 1/4 teaspoon black pepper
- 2 green onions, thinly sliced

Directions:

1. Peel the potatoes and cut them into 1-inch cubes.
2. Place the potato cubes in a large pot and cover with cold water. Add a pinch of salt.
3. Bring the water to a boil over high heat, then reduce the heat to medium-low and simmer for about 10-15 minutes or until the potatoes are tender when pierced with a fork.
4. Drain the cooked potatoes and let them cool for a few minutes.
5. In a separate bowl, whisk together the mayonnaise, Dijon mustard, white wine vinegar, salt, and black pepper. Add the sliced green onions and chopped parsley to the dressing.
6. Gently fold the dressing mixture into the cooked potatoes until well coated.
7. Taste and adjust the seasoning if needed.
8. Refrigerate the potato salad for at least 1 hour to allow the flavors to meld together.
9. Serve the Insalata di Patate chilled as a delicious side dish.

Nutritional Information (per serving): Calories: 250 Protein: 4g Carbohydrates: 35g Fat: 11g Fiber: 4g Cholesterol: 5mg Sodium: 450mg Potassium: 900mg

Insalata di Funghi (Mushroom Salad)

Yield: 4 servings | Prep time: 10 minutes | Cook time: 5 minutes

Ingredients:

- 8 ounces (225g) mushrooms, sliced
- 2 tablespoons extra virgin olive oil
- 1 tablespoon lemon juice
- Parmesan cheese, grated (for garnish)
- 1 garlic clove, minced
- 1/4 cup chopped fresh parsley
- Salt and pepper to taste

Directions:

1. Heat the olive oil in a skillet over medium heat.
2. Add the sliced mushrooms and sauté for 4-5 minutes until they become tender and lightly browned.
3. In a small bowl, whisk together the lemon juice, minced garlic, chopped parsley, salt, and pepper.
4. Transfer the cooked mushrooms to a mixing bowl and pour the lemon-garlic dressing over them.
5. Toss the mushrooms gently to coat them evenly with the dressing.
6. Let the mushroom salad marinate for at least 10 minutes to allow the flavors to meld together.
7. Before serving, garnish with grated Parmesan cheese for an extra touch of flavor.
8. Serve the Insalata di Funghi as a refreshing salad.

Nutritional Information (per serving): Calories: 70 Protein: 3g Carbohydrates: 4g Fat: 6g Fiber: 1g Cholesterol: 0mg Sodium: 10mg Potassium: 400mg

Insalata Verde (Green Salad)
Yield: 4 servings | Prep time: 10 minutes | Cook time: 15 minutes

Ingredients:

- 6 cups mixed salad greens (such as lettuce, spinach, arugula)
- 1 cucumber, sliced
- 1 small red onion, thinly sliced
- Salt and pepper to taste
- 1 cup cherry tomatoes, halved
- 1/4 cup Kalamata olives
- 2 tablespoons extra virgin olive oil
- 1 tablespoon balsamic vinegar

Directions:

1. In a large salad bowl, combine the mixed salad greens, cucumber slices, red onion slices, cherry tomatoes, and Kalamata olives.
2. In a small bowl, whisk together the extra virgin olive oil, balsamic vinegar, salt, and pepper to make the dressing.
3. Drizzle the dressing over the salad and toss gently to coat the ingredients evenly.
4. Adjust the seasoning if needed.
5. Serve the Insalata Verde immediately as a refreshing and light side dish or as a base for other toppings and dressings.
6. Enjoy!

Nutritional Information (per serving): Calories: 80 Protein: 2g Carbohydrates: 7g Fat: 6g Fiber: 2g Cholesterol: 0mg Sodium: 120mg Potassium: 300mg

Italian Soups dishes

Minestrone Soup

Yield: 4 servings | Prep time: 15 minutes | Cook time: 30 minutes

Ingredient list:

- 2 tablespoons olive oil
- 1 onion, diced
- 2 cloves garlic, minced
- 2 carrots, diced
- 2 celery stalks, diced
- 1 zucchini, diced
- Grated Parmesan cheese (for serving)
- 1 cup green beans, cut into 1-inch pieces
- 1 can (14 oz) diced tomatoes
- 4 cups vegetable broth
- 1 can (14 oz) cannellini beans, drained and rinsed
- 1/2 cup small pasta (such as ditalini or elbow)
- 1 teaspoon dried oregano
- 1 teaspoon dried basil
- Salt and pepper to taste

Directions:

1. In a large pot, heat the olive oil over medium heat. Add the diced onion and garlic, and cook until softened and fragrant. Add the diced carrots, celery, zucchini, and green beans to the pot. Cook for about 5 minutes, stirring occasionally. Pour in the diced tomatoes and vegetable broth. Bring the soup to a boil, then reduce the heat to low and let it simmer for 10 minutes. Add the cannellini beans and pasta to the pot. Cook until the pasta is tender, usually about 10 minutes. Season the soup with dried oregano, dried basil, salt, and pepper. Adjust the seasonings to your taste.

Nutritional Information: (per serving) Calories: 220 Protein: 8g Carbohydrates: 32g Fat: 7g Fiber: 8g Cholesterol: 0mg Sodium: 760mg Potassium: 590mg

Zuppa Toscana (Tuscan Soup)

Yield: 4 servings | Prep time: 10 minutes | Cook time: 30 minutes

Ingredient list:

- 1 tablespoon olive oil
- 1 pound Italian sausage, casings removed
- 1 onion, diced
- 3 cloves garlic, minced
- 4 cups chicken broth
- 3 cups water
- Grated Parmesan cheese (for serving
- 3 large potatoes, peeled and sliced
- 1 bunch kale, stems removed and leaves chopped
- 1 cup heavy cream
- Salt and pepper to taste

Directions:

1. Heat the olive oil in a large pot over medium heat. Add the Italian sausage and cook until browned, breaking it up into small pieces with a spoon. Add the diced onion and minced garlic to the pot. Cook until the onion is translucent and the garlic is fragrant. Pour in the chicken broth and water. Bring the soup to a boil, then reduce the heat to low and let it simmer for 10 minutes. Add the sliced potatoes to the pot. Cook until the potatoes are tender, about 15 minutes. Stir in the chopped kale and cook for an additional 5 minutes until wilted. Pour in the heavy cream and stir well. Season the soup with salt and pepper to taste.

Nutritional Information: (per serving) Calories: 460 Protein: 18g Carbohydrates: 27g Fat: 31g Fiber: 2g Cholesterol: 90mg Sodium: 1250mg Potassium: 770mg

Pasta e Fagioli (Pasta and Bean Soup)

Yield: 4 servings | Prep time: 10 minutes | Cook time: 30 minutes

Ingredient list:

- 2 tablespoons olive oil
- 1 onion, diced
- 2 cloves garlic, minced
- 2 carrots, diced
- 2 celery stalks, diced
- 1 can (14 ounces) diced tomatoes
- 4 cups vegetable broth
- 2 cups cooked cannellini beans
- 1 cup small pasta (such as ditalini or elbow macaroni)
- 1 teaspoon dried oregano
- 1 teaspoon dried basil
- Salt and pepper to taste
- Grated Parmesan cheese (for serving)

Directions:

1. Heat the olive oil in a large pot over medium heat. Add the diced onion, minced garlic, diced carrots, and diced celery. Cook until the vegetables are softened. Add the diced tomatoes with their juice to the pot. Stir in the vegetable broth and bring the soup to a boil. Reduce the heat to low and add the cooked cannellini beans to the pot. Simmer for 10 minutes. In a separate pot, cook the pasta according to the package instructions until al dente. Drain and set aside. Add the cooked pasta to the soup. Stir in the dried oregano and dried basil. Season with salt and pepper to taste. Let the soup simmer for an additional 5 minutes to allow the flavors to meld together.

Nutritional Information: (per serving) Calories: 320 Protein: 11g Carbohydrates: 50g Fat: 8g Fiber: 8g Cholesterol: 0mg Sodium: 800mg Potassium: 650mg

Ribollita (Tuscan Vegetable Soup)

Yield: 4 servings | Prep time: 15 minutes | Cook time: 45 minutes

Ingredient list:

- 2 tablespoons olive oil
- 1 onion, chopped
- 2 carrots, diced
- 2 celery stalks, diced
- 3 cloves garlic, minced
- 1 can (14 ounces) diced tomatoes
- 4 cups vegetable broth
- 2 cups chopped kale or Swiss chard
- 1 can (14 ounces) cannellini beans, drained and rinsed
- 1 cup stale bread, torn into small pieces
- 1 teaspoon dried thyme
- Salt and pepper to taste
- Grated Parmesan cheese (for serving)

Directions:

1. Heat the olive oil in a large pot over medium heat. Add the chopped onion, diced carrots, diced celery, and minced garlic. Cook until the vegetables are softened. Stir in the diced tomatoes with their juice and the vegetable broth. Bring the soup to a boil, then reduce the heat to low. Add the chopped kale or Swiss chard to the pot and simmer for 20 minutes until the greens are tender. Add the cannellini beans and torn bread to the pot. Stir well to combine and let the soup simmer for another 10 minutes.
2. Season the soup with dried thyme, salt, and pepper to taste. Adjust the seasonings according to your preference. Remove the pot from the heat and let the Ribollita rest for a few minutes before serving.

Nutritional Information: (per serving) Calories: 280 Protein: 10g Carbohydrates: 42g Fat: 8g Fiber: 10g Cholesterol: 0mg Sodium: 800mg Potassium: 760mg

Zuppa di Pesce (Italian Fish Soup)

Yield: 4 servings | Prep time: 20 minutes | Cook time: 30 minutes

Ingredient list:

- 2 tablespoons olive oil
- 1 onion, chopped
- 3 cloves garlic, minced
- 1 red bell pepper, sliced
- 1 fennel bulb, sliced
- 1 can (14 ounces) diced tomatoes
- 4 cups fish or vegetable broth
- 1 cup dry white wine
- Fresh parsley, chopped (for garnish)

- 1 teaspoon dried oregano
- 1/2 teaspoon red pepper flakes (optional)
- 1 bay leaf
- 1 pound mixed fish and seafood (such as shrimp, mussels, clams, squid), cleaned and deveined
- Salt and pepper to taste

Directions:

1. Heat the olive oil in a large pot over medium heat. Add the chopped onion and minced garlic. Cook until the onion becomes translucent. Add the sliced red bell pepper and fennel to the pot. Sauté for a few minutes until the vegetables are slightly softened. Stir in the diced tomatoes, fish or vegetable broth, and white wine. Add the dried oregano, red pepper flakes (if using), and bay leaf. Bring the soup to a simmer.
2. Reduce the heat to low and let the soup simmer for 15 minutes to allow the flavors to meld together.
3. Add the mixed fish and seafood to the pot. Cook for 5-7 minutes or until the fish is cooked through and the seafood has opened (discard any unopened shells). Season the soup with salt and pepper to taste. Adjust the seasonings according to your preference. Remove the bay leaf from the soup. Ladle the Zuppa di Pesce into bowls and garnish with fresh chopped parsley.

Nutritional Information: (per serving) Calories: 280 Protein: 30g Carbohydrates: 10g Fat: 10g Fiber: 2g Cholesterol: 120mg Sodium: 900mg Potassium: 600mg

Stracciatella Soup

Yield: 4 servings | Prep time: 10 minutes | Cook time: 15 minutes

Ingredient list:

- 4 cups chicken or vegetable broth
- 2 large eggs
- 1/4 cup grated Parmesan cheese
- Grated nutmeg (optional)

- 2 tablespoons fresh parsley, chopped
- Salt and pepper to taste

Directions:

1. In a medium saucepan, bring the chicken or vegetable broth to a simmer over medium heat.
2. In a bowl, whisk together the eggs, grated Parmesan cheese, and chopped parsley. Season with salt and pepper to taste. Add a pinch of grated nutmeg if desired. Slowly pour the egg mixture into the simmering broth, stirring gently with a fork to create thin strands of cooked egg. Cook the soup for 2-3 minutes, stirring occasionally, until the egg is fully cooked and the soup is slightly thickened. Taste the soup and adjust the seasoning with salt and pepper if needed. Ladle the Stracciatella Soup into bowls and serve hot.

Nutritional Information: (per serving) Calories: 120 Protein: 10g Carbohydrates: 3g Fat: 7g Fiber: 0g Cholesterol: 115mg Sodium: 800mg Potassium: 200mg

Italian Wedding Soup

Yield: 4 servings | Prep time: 20 minutes | Cook time: 25 minutes

Ingredient list:

- 1/2 pound ground beef
- 1/2 cup breadcrumbs
- 1/4 cup grated Parmesan cheese
- 1/4 cup fresh parsley, chopped
- 1 egg, lightly beaten
- 1 small onion, finely chopped
- Salt and pepper to taste

- 2 cloves garlic, minced
- 6 cups chicken broth
- 1 cup acini di pepe pasta or small pasta of your choice
- 4 cups fresh spinach, chopped

Directions:

1. In a bowl, combine the ground beef, breadcrumbs, grated Parmesan cheese, chopped parsley, and lightly beaten egg. Mix well to combine. Roll the mixture into small meatballs, about 1 inch in diameter.
2. In a large pot, heat some olive oil over medium heat. Add the chopped onion and minced garlic, and cook until softened. Add the chicken broth to the pot and bring it to a boil. Gently drop the meatballs into the boiling broth and cook for about 10 minutes, or until the meatballs are cooked through. Stir in the acini di pepe pasta and cook for an additional 8-10 minutes, or until the pasta is tender. Add the chopped spinach to the soup and cook for 2-3 minutes, or until wilted. Season the soup with salt and pepper to taste.
3. Serve the Italian Wedding Soup hot, garnished with additional grated Parmesan cheese if desired.

Nutritional Information: (per serving) Calories: 320 Protein: 20g Carbohydrates: 30g Fat: 12g Fiber: 3g Cholesterol: 90mg Sodium: 1100mg Potassium: 600mg

Cacciucco (Tuscan Seafood Stew)

Yield: 4 servings | Prep time: 15 minutes | Cook time: 40 minutes

Ingredients:

- 1 lb mixed seafood (such as shrimp, mussels, clams, calamari)
- 2 tbsp olive oil
- 1 onion, chopped
- 2 cloves garlic, minced
- 1 carrot, diced
- Fresh parsley, for garnish

- 1 stalk celery, diced
- 1 can (14 oz) diced tomatoes
- 1 cup fish or vegetable broth
- 1/2 cup dry white wine
- 1/2 tsp red pepper flakes
- Salt and pepper, to taste

Directions:

1. Heat olive oil in a large pot over medium heat. Add the chopped onion, minced garlic, diced carrot, and diced celery. Sauté until vegetables are softened, about 5 minutes.
2. Add the diced tomatoes, fish or vegetable broth, and white wine to the pot. Bring to a simmer.
3. Add the mixed seafood and red pepper flakes to the pot. Season with salt and pepper.
4. Cover the pot and let the stew simmer for about 20-25 minutes, or until the seafood is cooked through and the flavors have melded together. Taste and adjust the seasoning if needed. Serve hot.

Nutritional Information (per serving): Calories: 250 Protein: 25g Carbohydrates: 10g Fat: 10g Fiber: 2g Cholesterol: 120mg Sodium: 600mg Potassium: 400mg

Zuppa di Lenticchie (Lentil Soup)

Yield: 4 servings | Prep time: 10 minutes | Cook time: 30 minutes

Ingredients:

- 1 cup dried lentils
- 2 tbsp olive oil
- 1 onion, chopped
- 2 cloves garlic, minced
- 2 carrots, diced
- 2 stalks celery, diced
- Fresh parsley, for garnish

- 1 can (14 oz) diced tomatoes
- 4 cups vegetable broth
- 1 tsp dried thyme
- 1 tsp dried oregano
- Salt and pepper, to taste

Directions:

1. Rinse the dried lentils and set aside. Heat olive oil in a large pot over medium heat.
2. Add the chopped onion, minced garlic, diced carrots, and diced celery. Sauté until vegetables are softened, about 5 minutes. Add the diced tomatoes (with their juice), vegetable broth, dried thyme, dried oregano, and rinsed lentils to the pot. Stir to combine. Bring the soup to a boil, then reduce heat to low and simmer for about 25-30 minutes, or until the lentils are tender. Season with salt and pepper to taste.
3. Serve the Zuppa di Lenticchie hot, garnished with fresh parsley.

Nutritional Information (per serving): Calories: 280 Protein: 15g Carbohydrates: 45g Fat: 6g Fiber: 15g Cholesterol: 0mg Sodium: 800mg Potassium: 1200mg

Farinata Soup

Yield: 4 servings | Prep time: 15 minutes | Cook time: 40 minutes

Ingredients:

- 1 cup chickpea flour
- 2 cups water
- 2 tbsp olive oil
- 1 onion, chopped
- 2 cloves garlic, minced
- 2 carrots, diced
- Fresh parsley, for garnish

- 2 stalks celery, diced
- 1 can (14 oz) diced tomatoes
- 4 cups vegetable broth
- 1 tsp dried basil
- 1 tsp dried thyme
- Salt and pepper, to taste

Directions:

1. In a bowl, whisk together chickpea flour and water until smooth. Set aside to rest for 30 minutes.
2. Heat olive oil in a large pot over medium heat. Add the chopped onion, minced garlic, diced carrots, and diced celery. Sauté until vegetables are softened, about 5 minutes.
3. Add the diced tomatoes (with their juice), vegetable broth, dried basil, and dried thyme to the pot. Stir to combine. Bring the soup to a boil, then reduce heat to low and simmer for 20 minutes.
4. Slowly pour the chickpea flour mixture into the soup while stirring continuously to prevent lumps from forming. Continue simmering for another 10 minutes, stirring occasionally, until the soup thickens.
5. Season with salt and pepper to taste. Serve the Farinata Soup hot, garnished with fresh parsley.

Nutritional Information (per serving): Calories: 220 Protein: 10g Carbohydrates: 35g Fat: 6g Fiber: 8g Cholesterol: 0mg Sodium: 800mg Potassium: 700mg

Tortellini in Brodo (Tortellini Soup)

Yield: 4 servings | Prep time: 10 minutes | Cook time: 20 minutes

Ingredients:

- 8 oz tortellini (cheese or meat-filled)
- 4 cups chicken or vegetable broth
- 1 carrot, diced
- 1 stalk celery, diced
- 1/2 onion, chopped
- Grated Parmesan cheese, for serving (optional)
- 2 cloves garlic, minced
- 1 tbsp olive oil
- 1 tsp dried thyme
- Salt and pepper, to taste
- Fresh parsley, for garnish

Directions:

1. In a large pot, heat olive oil over medium heat. Add the chopped onion, minced garlic, diced carrot, and diced celery. Sauté until vegetables are softened, about 5 minutes. Pour the chicken or vegetable broth into the pot. Add the dried thyme and season with salt and pepper. Bring the broth to a boil, then reduce heat to low and simmer for 10 minutes to allow the flavors to meld. Meanwhile, cook the tortellini according to the package instructions. Drain and set aside. Once the broth is ready, add the cooked tortellini to the pot. Stir gently to combine. Simmer for another 5 minutes to heat the tortellini through. Taste and adjust the seasoning if needed. Serve garnished with fresh parsley and grated Parmesan cheese if desired.

Nutritional Information (per serving): Calories: 300 Protein: 15g Carbohydrates: 40g Fat: 8g Fiber: 4g Cholesterol: 30mg Sodium: 1000mg Potassium: 350mg

Pappa al Pomodoro (Tomato Bread Soup)

Yield: 4 servings | Prep time: 15 minutes | Cook time: 30 minutes

Ingredients:

- 4 cups day-old bread, torn into small pieces
- 4 cups ripe tomatoes, peeled and chopped
- 1 onion, chopped
- 2 cloves garlic, minced
- 2 tbsp olive oil
- Grated Parmesan cheese, for serving (optional)
- 4 cups vegetable broth
- 1 tsp dried basil
- 1 tsp dried oregano
- Salt and pepper, to taste
- Fresh basil leaves, for garnish

Directions:

1. In a large pot, heat olive oil over medium heat. Add the chopped onion and minced garlic. Sauté until the onion becomes translucent, about 5 minutes. Add the chopped tomatoes to the pot. Stir and cook for another 5 minutes until the tomatoes start to break down. Add the torn bread pieces to the pot, along with the vegetable broth, dried basil, dried oregano, salt, and pepper. Stir well to combine and bring the soup to a simmer. Reduce heat to low and cover the pot. Let the soup simmer for about 20 minutes, stirring occasionally, until the bread absorbs the flavors and becomes soft. If desired, use an immersion blender to partially puree the soup for a smoother texture. Taste and adjust the seasoning if needed. Serve garnished with fresh basil leaves and grated Parmesan cheese if desired.

Nutritional Information (per serving): Calories: 250 Protein: 5g Carbohydrates: 40g Fat: 8g Fiber: 5g Cholesterol: 0mg Sodium: 800mg Potassium: 550mg

Zuppa di Cipolle (Onion Soup)

Yield: 4 servings | Prep time: 10 minutes | Cook time: 40 minutes

Ingredients:

- 4 large onions, thinly sliced
- 2 tbsp butter
- 2 tbsp olive oil
- 4 cups beef or vegetable broth
- 1/2 cup dry white wine
- 1 cup shredded Gruyere or Swiss cheese
- 1 tsp sugar
- 1 tsp dried thyme
- Salt and pepper, to taste
- 4 slices of crusty bread

Directions:

1. In a large pot, melt the butter with the olive oil over medium heat. Add the sliced onions to the pot and cook, stirring occasionally, until they become soft and caramelized, about 30 minutes. Stir in the sugar to help enhance the caramelization process. Pour in the white wine and cook for a couple of minutes to deglaze the pot. Add the beef or vegetable broth and dried thyme to the pot. Season with salt and pepper to taste. Bring the soup to a boil, then reduce heat to low and let it simmer for 10 minutes to allow the flavors to meld together. Meanwhile, toast the slices of crusty bread until golden and crispy.
2. Ladle the hot soup into oven-safe bowls. Place a slice of toasted bread on top of each bowl.
3. Sprinkle a generous amount of shredded Gruyere or Swiss cheese over the bread slices.
4. Place the bowls under the broiler for a few minutes until the cheese is melted and bubbly.
5. Carefully remove the bowls from the oven and let them cool slightly before serving.

Nutritional Information (per serving): Calories: 350 Protein: 12g Carbohydrates: 30g Fat: 20g Fiber: 4g Cholesterol: 40mg Sodium: 800mg Potassium: 400mg

Crema di Funghi (Creamy Mushroom Soup)

Yield: 4 servings | Prep time: 10 minutes | Cook time: 25 minutes

Ingredients:

- 1 lb fresh mushrooms, sliced
- 2 tbsp butter
- 1 onion, chopped
- 2 cloves garlic, minced
- Fresh parsley, chopped (for garnish)
- 4 cups vegetable or chicken broth
- 1 cup heavy cream
- 1 tsp dried thyme
- Salt and pepper, to taste

Directions:

1. In a large pot, melt the butter over medium heat. Add the chopped onion and minced garlic. Sauté until the onion becomes translucent, about 5 minutes. Add the sliced mushrooms to the pot and cook until they release their moisture and start to brown, about 8-10 minutes. Pour in the vegetable or chicken broth and add the dried thyme. Bring the mixture to a boil, then reduce heat to low and simmer for 10 minutes.
2. Using an immersion blender or a regular blender, puree the soup until smooth and creamy.
3. Return the soup to the pot and stir in the heavy cream. Season with salt and pepper to taste.
4. Heat the soup over low heat, stirring occasionally, until it is heated through.
5. Ladle the creamy mushroom soup into bowls and garnish with fresh parsley. Serve hot and enjoy!

Nutritional Information (per serving): Calories: 200 Protein: 5g Carbohydrates: 12g Fat: 16g Fiber: 2g Cholesterol: 60mg Sodium: 800mg Potassium: 450mg

Brodo di Carne (Italian Meat Broth)

Yield: 4 servings | Prep time: 10 minutes | Cook time: 2 hours

Ingredients:

- 1 lb beef bones
- 1 lb chicken bones
- 1 onion, quartered
- 2 carrots, chopped
- 2 celery stalks, chopped
- Salt and pepper, to taste
- 4 cloves garlic, crushed
- 1 bay leaf
- 1 sprig fresh rosemary
- 1 sprig fresh thyme
- 10 cups water

Directions:

1. Preheat the oven to 400°F (200°C). Place the beef and chicken bones on a baking sheet and roast them in the oven for 30 minutes until they are browned. In a large pot, combine the roasted bones, onion, carrots, celery, garlic, bay leaf, rosemary, thyme, and water.
2. Bring the mixture to a boil over high heat, then reduce the heat to low and simmer, partially covered, for 2 hours. Skim off any foam or impurities that rise to the surface of the broth.
3. After 2 hours, remove the pot from the heat and strain the broth through a fine-mesh sieve into another pot or large bowl. Discard the solids and return the strained broth to the stove. Season with salt and pepper to taste. Bring the broth to a simmer and let it cook for another 10 minutes to enhance the flavors.
4. Remove from heat and let the broth cool slightly before serving.
5. Ladle the Italian meat broth into bowls and serve it hot as a comforting and nourishing soup on its own or as a base for other dishes.

Nutritional Information (per serving): Calories: 100 Protein: 12g Carbohydrates: 4g Fat: 4g Fiber: 1g Cholesterol: 25mg Sodium: 500mg Potassium: 400mg

Italian Pasta dishes.

Spaghetti Bolognese

Yield: 4 servings | Prep time: 15 minutes | Cook time: 45 minutes

Ingredients:

- 8 oz spaghetti
- 1 lb ground beef
- Onion, garlic, carrot, celery
- Parmesan cheese, fresh basil leaves
- Crushed tomatoes, tomato paste
- Beef broth, red wine (optional)
- Oregano, basil, salt, pepper

Directions:

1. Cook spaghetti.
2. Brown ground beef with onion and garlic.
3. Add carrot, celery, cook briefly.
4. Pour in tomatoes, tomato paste, broth, and wine.
5. Season with herbs, salt, and pepper. Simmer.
6. Serve sauce over cooked spaghetti.
7. Garnish with Parmesan and basil.

Nutritional Information (per serving): Calories: 480 Protein: 21g Carbohydrates: 54g Fat: 18g Fiber: 6g Cholesterol: 47mg Sodium: 580mg Potassium: 850mg

Fettuccine Alfredo

Yield: 4 servings | Prep time: 10 minutes | Cook time: 15 minutes

Ingredients:

- 8 oz fettuccine pasta
- 1 cup heavy cream
- Salt, pepper, nutmeg
- 1/2 cup grated Parmesan cheese
- 2 tbsp unsalted butte

Directions:

1. Cook fettuccine according to package instructions.
2. Heat cream and butter in a saucepan.
3. Whisk in Parmesan cheese until smooth.
4. Season with salt, pepper, and nutmeg.
5. Simmer the sauce until thickened.
6. Drain pasta and add it to the sauce.
7. Toss well to coat the pasta.
8. Serve and enjoy!

Nutritional Information (per serving): Calories: 670 Protein: 17g Carbohydrates: 47g Fat: 47g Fiber: 2g Cholesterol: 196mg Sodium: 500mg Potassium: 230mg

Carbonara

Yield: 4 servings | Prep time: 10 minutes | Cook time: 15 minutes

Ingredients:

- 8 ounces (225g) spaghetti
- 4 ounces (115g) pancetta or bacon, diced
- 2 cloves garlic, minced
- Chopped parsley, for garnish (optional)

- 2 large eggs
- 1 cup (100g) grated Parmesan cheese
- Freshly ground black pepper, to taste

Directions:

1. Cook the spaghetti according to package instructions until al dente. Drain and set aside.
2. In a large skillet, cook the diced pancetta or bacon over medium heat until crispy. Remove from the skillet and set aside. In the same skillet, add the minced garlic and sauté for 1 minute until fragrant.
3. In a mixing bowl, whisk together the eggs, grated Parmesan cheese, and freshly ground black pepper.
4. Add the cooked spaghetti to the skillet with the garlic, then pour in the egg mixture. Toss well to coat the pasta evenly and cook for an additional 2-3 minutes, stirring constantly, until the sauce thickens slightly and coats the pasta. Stir in the cooked pancetta or bacon.
5. Serve the Carbonara hot, garnished with chopped parsley if desired.

Nutritional Information (per serving): Calories: 540 Protein: 25g Carbohydrates: 49g Fat: 26g Fiber: 2g Cholesterol: 195mg Sodium: 650mg Potassium: 250mg

Lasagna

Yield: 6 servings | Prep time: 30 minutes | Cook time: 1 hour

Ingredients:

- 12 lasagna noodles
- 1 lb ground beef
- 1/2 cup chopped onion
- 2 cloves garlic, minced
- 14 oz crushed tomatoes
- 6 oz tomato paste
- 1 tsp dried basil
- Chopped fresh parsley, for garnish (optional)

- 1 tsp dried oregano
- Salt and pepper to taste
- 2 cups ricotta cheese
- 1 egg, lightly beaten
- 2 cups shredded mozzarella cheese
- 1/2 cup grated Parmesan cheese

Directions:

1. Cook lasagna noodles, drain, and set aside.
2. Cook ground beef, onion, and garlic until browned. Drain excess fat.
3. Stir in crushed tomatoes, tomato paste, basil, oregano, salt, and pepper. Simmer for 10 minutes.
4. In a separate bowl, mix ricotta cheese and beaten egg.
5. Layer meat sauce, noodles, ricotta mixture, mozzarella, and Parmesan cheese in a 9x13-inch baking dish.
6. Repeat the layers, ending with meat sauce and cheese on top. Cover with foil and bake at 375°F (190°C) for 40 minutes. Remove foil and bake for an additional 10 minutes until cheese is golden.
7. Let it rest before serving. Garnish with parsley, if desired.

Nutritional Information (per serving): Calories: 610 Protein: 37g Carbohydrates: 51g Fat: 28g Fiber: 3g Cholesterol: 130mg Sodium: 900mg Potassium: 740mg

Ravioli

Yield: 4 servings | Prep time: 30 minutes | Cook time: 10 minutes

Ingredients:

- 1 package (20 ounces/565g) refrigerated or frozen ravioli
- 2 tablespoons olive oil
- 2 cloves garlic, minced
- 1 can (14 ounces/400g) diced tomatoes
- 1/2 teaspoon dried basil
- 1/2 teaspoon dried oregano
- Salt and pepper to taste
- Grated Parmesan cheese, for serving
- Chopped fresh basil, for garnish (optional)

Directions:

1. Cook the ravioli according to package instructions. Drain and set aside. In a large skillet, heat the olive oil over medium heat. Add the minced garlic and sauté for 1 minute until fragrant.
2. Add the diced tomatoes, dried basil, dried oregano, salt, and pepper to the skillet. Stir well and simmer for 5 minutes.
3. Gently stir in the cooked ravioli and cook for an additional 2-3 minutes, allowing the flavors to combine.
4. Remove from heat and serve the ravioli hot. Sprinkle with grated Parmesan cheese and garnish with chopped fresh basil, if desired.

Nutritional Information (per serving): Calories: 430 Protein: 16g Carbohydrates: 54g Fat: 16g Fiber: 4g Cholesterol: 45mg Sodium: 650mg Potassium: 220mg

Penne Arrabiata

Yield: 4 servings | Prep time: 10 minutes | Cook time: 20 minutes

Ingredients:

- 8 ounces (225g) penne pasta
- 2 tablespoons olive oil
- 4 cloves garlic, minced
- 1/2 teaspoon crushed red pepper flakes (adjust to taste)
- 1 can (14 ounces/400g) diced tomatoes
- Fresh basil leaves, for garnish (optional)
- 1/4 cup (60ml) tomato paste
- 1 teaspoon dried basil
- 1 teaspoon dried oregano
- Salt and pepper to taste
- Grated Parmesan cheese, for serving

Directions:

1. Cook the penne pasta according to package instructions until al dente. Drain and set aside.
2. In a large skillet, heat the olive oil over medium heat. Add the minced garlic and crushed red pepper flakes. Sauté for 1 minute until fragrant. Add the diced tomatoes, tomato paste, dried basil, dried oregano, salt, and pepper to the skillet. Stir well and simmer for 10 minutes, allowing the flavors to meld together.
3. Add the cooked penne pasta to the skillet and toss to coat the pasta with the sauce. Cook for an additional 2-3 minutes to heat through.
4. Remove from heat and serve the Penne Arrabiata hot. Sprinkle with grated Parmesan cheese and garnish with fresh basil leaves, if desired.

Nutritional Information (per serving): Calories: 370 Protein: 9g Carbohydrates: 64g Fat: 8g Fiber: 5g Cholesterol: 0mg Sodium: 520mg Potassium: 470mg

Linguine with Clam Sauce

Yield: 4 servings | Prep time: 10 minutes | Cook time: 20 minutes

Ingredients:

- 8 oz linguine pasta
- 2 tbsp olive oil
- 4 cloves garlic, minced
- 1/2 tsp red pepper flakes
- 10 oz canned baby clams, drained (reserve juice)
- Lemon wedges, for serving (optional)

- 1/2 cup dry white wine
- 1/4 cup clam juice
- 1 tbsp butter
- 2 tbsp chopped fresh parsley
- Salt and pepper to taste
- Grated Parmesan cheese, for serving

Directions:

1. Cook linguine according to package instructions. Drain and set aside.
2. Heat olive oil in a skillet. Sauté garlic and red pepper flakes for 1 minute.
3. Add clams and cook for 2 minutes. Pour in white wine and clam juice. Simmer for 5 minutes.
4. Stir in butter, parsley, salt, and pepper.
5. Add cooked linguine to the skillet and toss to coat.
6. Cook for 2-3 minutes to heat through.
7. Serve linguine with clam sauce, topped with Parmesan cheese.
8. Serve with lemon wedges, if desired.

Nutritional Information (per serving): Calories: 430 Protein: 14g Carbohydrates: 62g Fat: 11g Fiber: 3g Cholesterol: 32mg Sodium: 570mg Potassium: 220mg

Tortellini Carbonara

Yield: 4 servings | Prep time: 10 minutes | Cook time: 15 minutes

Ingredients:

- 9 oz cheese tortellini
- 4 slices bacon, diced
- 3 cloves garlic, minced
- 2 large eggs
- Chopped fresh parsley, for garnish (optional)

- 1/2 cup heavy cream
- 1/2 cup grated Parmesan cheese
- Salt and black pepper to taste

Directions:

1. Cook tortellini according to package instructions. Drain and set aside.
2. Cook diced bacon until crispy. Remove and set aside, reserving the bacon fat in the skillet.
3. Sauté minced garlic in the skillet for 1 minute. In a bowl, whisk eggs, cream, Parmesan cheese, salt, and pepper. Add tortellini to the skillet and toss in the bacon fat.
4. Pour the egg mixture over the tortellini, stirring quickly to cook the eggs.
5. Add cooked bacon back to the skillet and stir.
6. Remove from heat and let rest for a few minutes.
7. Serve Tortellini Carbonara hot, garnished with parsley if desired.

Nutritional Information (per serving): Calories: 570 Protein: 25g Carbohydrates: 44g Fat: 33g Fiber: 3g Cholesterol: 215mg Sodium: 810mg Potassium: 260mg

Pappardelle with Wild Mushroom Sauce

Yield: 4 servings | Prep time: 15 minutes | Cook time: 20 minutes

Ingredients:

- 12 oz pappardelle pasta
- 2 tbsp olive oil
- 1 medium onion, finely chopped
- 2 cloves garlic, minced
- 12 oz mixed wild mushrooms, sliced
- 1/2 cup vegetable broth
- 1/2 cup heavy cream
- 1/4 cup grated Parmesan cheese
- 2 tbsp chopped fresh parsley
- Salt and pepper to taste

Directions:

1. Cook pappardelle pasta according to package instructions. Drain and set aside.
2. Sauté onion and garlic in olive oil until softened.
3. Add sliced wild mushrooms and cook until tender.
4. Pour in vegetable broth and simmer for 5 minutes.
5. Stir in heavy cream and simmer for 2-3 minutes.
6. Add cooked pappardelle pasta to the skillet and toss to coat with the sauce.
7. Stir in Parmesan cheese and parsley. Season with salt and pepper.
8. Let the sauce thicken for a few minutes off the heat.
9. Serve Pappardelle with Wild Mushroom Sauce hot, garnished as desired.

Nutritional Information (per serving): Calories: 480 Protein: 13g Carbohydrates: 63g Fat: 19g Fiber: 4g Cholesterol: 45mg Sodium: 320mg Potassium: 440mg

Orecchiette with Broccoli Rabe and Sausage

Yield: 4 servings | Prep time: 10 minutes | Cook time: 25 minutes

Ingredients:

- 12 oz orecchiette pasta
- 1 bunch broccoli rabe, chopped
- 8 oz Italian sausage, casings removed
- 3 cloves garlic, minced
- Grated Parmesan cheese for serving (optional)
- 1/4 tsp red pepper flakes (optional)
- 2 tbsp olive oil
- 1/4 cup chicken broth
- Salt and black pepper to taste

Directions:

1. Cook orecchiette pasta according to package instructions.
2. Cook Italian sausage until browned; set aside.
3. Sauté garlic and red pepper flakes in olive oil.
4. Add broccoli rabe and cook until wilted.
5. Pour in chicken broth and simmer until tender.
6. Return sausage to skillet and combine with broccoli rabe.
7. Add cooked pasta and toss to coat.
8. Season with salt and pepper.
9. Serve Orecchiette with Broccoli Rabe and Sausage hot, with Parmesan cheese on top if desired.

Nutritional Information (per serving): Calories: 490 Protein: 19g Carbohydrates: 54g Fat: 23g Fiber: 4g Cholesterol: 40mg Sodium: 780mg Potassium: 480mg

Gnocchi alla Sorrentina

Yield: 4 servings | Prep time: 20 minutes | Cook time: 25 minutes

Ingredients:

- 1 lb potato gnocchi
- 2 cups marinara sauce
- 8 oz fresh mozzarella, diced
- 1/4 cup grated Parmesan cheese
- Fresh basil leaves
- Salt and black pepper to taste

Directions:

1. Cook gnocchi according to package instructions.
2. Preheat oven to 375°F (190°C).
3. Layer marinara sauce, cooked gnocchi, and diced mozzarella in a baking dish.
4. Sprinkle with Parmesan cheese, salt, and pepper.
5. Bake for 20 minutes until cheese melts and bubbles.
6. Garnish with torn basil leaves.
7. Serve Gnocchi alla Sorrentina hot, with additional Parmesan cheese if desired

Nutritional Information (per serving): Calories: 480 Protein: 18g Carbohydrates: 61g Fat: 18g Fiber: 4g Cholesterol: 40mg Sodium: 1100mg Potassium: 550mg

Tagliatelle with Pesto Genovese

Yield: 4 servings | Prep time: 10 minutes | Cook time: 10 minutes

Ingredients:

- 12 oz tagliatelle pasta
- 2 cups fresh basil leaves
- 1/2 cup grated Parmesan cheese
- 1/4 cup pine nuts
- 2 cloves garlic
- 1/2 cup extra-virgin olive oil
- Salt and black pepper to taste
- Grated Parmesan cheese for serving (optional

Directions:

1. Cook tagliatelle pasta according to package instructions.
2. In a food processor, combine basil, Parmesan cheese, pine nuts, and garlic. Pulse until finely chopped.
3. With the food processor running, slowly drizzle in olive oil until well combined and smooth. Season with salt and pepper.
4. Drain cooked pasta and return to the pot.
5. Add the pesto sauce to the pasta and toss until evenly coated.
6. Serve Tagliatelle with Pesto Genovese hot, garnished with additional grated Parmesan cheese if desired.

Nutritional Information (per serving): Calories: 560 Protein: 15g Carbohydrates: 58g Fat: 31g Fiber: 3g Cholesterol: 10mg Sodium: 320mg Potassium: 280mg

Cannelloni

Yield: 4 servings | Prep time: 30 minutes | Cook time: 30 minutes

Ingredients:

- 8 cannelloni tubes
- 1 lb ground beef
- 1/2 onion, finely chopped
- 2 cloves garlic, minced
- 1 cup ricotta cheese
- Fresh basil leaves for garnish
- 1 cup shredded mozzarella cheese
- 1/2 cup grated Parmesan cheese
- 2 cups marinara sauce
- 1 tablespoon olive oil
- Salt and black pepper to taste

Directions:

1. Cook cannelloni tubes and set aside.
2. Sauté onion and garlic, add ground beef, and cook until browned. Season with salt and pepper.
3. Combine beef mixture with ricotta, mozzarella, and half of Parmesan.
4. Stuff cannelloni tubes with the beef and cheese mixture.
5. Spread marinara sauce in a baking dish. Place stuffed cannelloni tubes in the dish.
6. Pour remaining marinara sauce over cannelloni and sprinkle with remaining cheeses.
7. Bake covered at 375°F (190°C) for 20 minutes.
8. Uncover and bake for another 10 minutes until cheese melts.
9. Garnish with fresh basil leaves.

Nutritional Information (per serving): Calories: 620 Protein: 38g Carbohydrates: 32g Fat: 38g Fiber: 3g Cholesterol: 130mg Sodium: 1050mg Potassium: 600mg

Farfalle with Tomato and Basil

Yield: 4 servings | Prep time: 10 minutes | Cook time: 20 minutes

Ingredients:

- 12 ounces farfalle pasta
- 2 tablespoons olive oil
- 3 cloves garlic, minced
- 1 can (14 ounces) diced tomatoes
- 1/4 teaspoon red pepper flakes
- Salt and black pepper to taste
- 1/4 cup fresh basil leaves, chopped
- Grated Parmesan cheese for serving

Directions:

1. Cook the farfalle pasta according to the package instructions. Drain and set aside.
2. Heat olive oil in a large skillet over medium heat. Add the minced garlic and sauté until fragrant.
3. Add the diced tomatoes and red pepper flakes to the skillet. Season with salt and black pepper. Cook for 10 minutes, stirring occasionally.
4. Add the cooked farfalle pasta to the skillet and toss to coat it evenly with the tomato sauce.
5. Stir in the chopped basil leaves and cook for an additional 2-3 minutes.
6. Remove from heat and serve the farfalle with a sprinkle of grated Parmesan cheese on top.

Nutritional Information (per serving): Calories: 360 Protein: 10g Carbohydrates: 60g Fat: 8g Fiber: 4g Cholesterol: 0mg Sodium: 320mg Potassium: 450mg

Cacio e Pepe

Yield: 4 servings | Prep time: 5 minutes | Cook time: 15 minutes

Ingredients:

- 12 ounces spaghetti
- 1 cup grated Pecorino Romano cheese
- Salt to taste

- 1 tablespoon freshly ground black pepper

Directions:

1. Cook the spaghetti in a large pot of salted boiling water until al dente. Drain, reserving 1/2 cup of the pasta water.
2. In a separate bowl, mix the grated Pecorino Romano cheese and black pepper.
3. Heat a large skillet over medium heat. Add the cooked spaghetti and a splash of the reserved pasta water.
4. Sprinkle the cheese and black pepper mixture over the spaghetti. Toss the pasta vigorously to melt the cheese and create a creamy sauce. If needed, add more pasta water to achieve the desired consistency.
5. Season with salt to taste, keeping in mind that the Pecorino Romano cheese is already salty.
6. Serve the Cacio e Pepe immediately, garnished with an extra sprinkle of black pepper.

Nutritional Information (per serving): Calories: 450 Protein: 20g Carbohydrates: 65g Fat: 12g Fiber: 3g
Cholesterol: 40mg Sodium: 550mg Potassium: 200mg

Pizza & Snacks dishes.

Margherita Pizza

Yield: 4 servings | Prep time: 15 minutes | Cook time: 12-15 minutes

Ingredients:

- 1 pizza dough (store-bought or homemade)
- 1 cup tomato sauce
- 8 ounces fresh mozzarella cheese, sliced
- Salt and pepper to taste
- Fresh basil leaves
- Olive oil

Directions:

1. Preheat your oven to the highest temperature setting (usually around 475-500°F or 245-260°C).
2. Roll out the pizza dough into a round shape on a floured surface, about 12 inches (30 cm) in diameter.
3. Transfer the dough to a pizza stone or baking sheet lined with parchment paper.
4. Spread the tomato sauce evenly over the dough, leaving a small border around the edges.
5. Arrange the mozzarella slices on top of the sauce. Tear some fresh basil leaves and distribute them over the pizza. Drizzle a little olive oil over the pizza and season with salt and pepper to taste.
6. Place the pizza in the preheated oven and bake for 12-15 minutes, or until the crust is golden brown and the cheese has melted and bubbled.
7. Remove the pizza from the oven and let it cool for a few minutes before slicing and serving.

Nutritional Information (per serving): Calories: 300 Protein: 12g Carbohydrates: 36g Fat: 12g Fiber: 2g Cholesterol: 20mg Sodium: 550mg Potassium: 200mg

Pepperoni Pizza

Yield: 4 servings | Prep time: 20 minutes | Cook time: 12-15 minutes

Ingredients:

- 1 pizza dough (store-bought or homemade)
- 1 cup tomato sauce
- 2 cups shredded mozzarella cheese
- Salt and pepper to taste
- 30-40 slices of pepperoni
- Olive oil
- Dried oregano

Directions:

1. Preheat your oven to the highest temperature setting (usually around 475-500°F or 245-260°C).
2. Roll out the pizza dough into a round shape on a floured surface, about 12 inches (30 cm) in diameter.
3. Transfer the dough to a pizza stone or baking sheet lined with parchment paper.
4. Spread the tomato sauce evenly over the dough, leaving a small border around the edges.
5. Sprinkle the shredded mozzarella cheese over the sauce, covering the entire surface.
6. Arrange the pepperoni slices on top of the cheese. Drizzle a little olive oil over the pizza and sprinkle with dried oregano, salt, and pepper to taste. Place the pizza in the preheated oven and bake for 12-15 minutes, or until the crust is golden brown and the cheese has melted and become bubbly.
7. Remove the pizza from the oven and let it cool for a few minutes before slicing and serving.

Nutritional Information (per serving): Calories: 380 Protein: 18g Carbohydrates: 32g Fat: 20g Fiber: 2g Cholesterol: 45mg Sodium: 980mg Potassium: 250mg

Caprese Pizza

Yield: 4 servings | Prep time: 15 minutes | Cook time: 12 minutes

Ingredients:

- 1 pizza dough (store-bought or homemade)
- 1 cup cherry tomatoes, sliced
- 8 ounces fresh mozzarella cheese, sliced
- Fresh basil leaves
- Salt and pepper to taste
- 2 cloves garlic, minced
- 2 tablespoons balsamic glaze
- Olive oil

Directions:

1. Preheat your oven to the highest temperature setting (usually around 475-500°F or 245-260°C).
2. Roll out the pizza dough into a round shape on a floured surface, about 12 inches (30 cm) in diameter.
3. Transfer the dough to a pizza stone or baking sheet lined with parchment paper.
4. Drizzle some olive oil over the dough and spread the minced garlic evenly.
5. Arrange the sliced mozzarella cheese and cherry tomatoes on top of the dough.
6. Season with salt and pepper to taste. Place the pizza in the preheated oven and bake for 12 minutes, or until the crust is golden brown and the cheese has melted.
7. Remove the pizza from the oven and let it cool for a minute.
8. Garnish with fresh basil leaves and drizzle balsamic glaze over the top.
9. Slice the pizza and serve immediately.

Nutritional Information (per serving): Calories: 340 Protein: 15g Carbohydrates: 35g Fat: 15g Fiber: 2g Cholesterol: 30mg Sodium: 450mg Potassium: 200mg

Quattro Formaggi Pizza

Yield: 4 servings | Prep time: 20 minutes | Cook time: 15 minutes

Ingredients:

- 1 pizza dough
- 1 cup mozzarella cheese
- 1/2 cup gorgonzola cheese
- 1/2 cup Parmesan cheese
- 1/2 cup Fontina cheese
- 1/4 cup pizza sauce
- 2 cloves garlic, minced
- Fresh basil leaves, for garnish (optional)

Directions:

1. Preheat oven to 450°F (230°C) with a pizza stone or baking sheet inside.
2. Roll out dough and transfer to a pizza peel or lined baking sheet.
3. Spread pizza sauce and sprinkle minced garlic over the dough.
4. Scatter the four cheeses evenly.
5. Transfer the pizza to the preheated oven.
6. Bake for 12-15 minutes until golden and bubbly.
7. Let it cool slightly, then slice and serve.
8. Garnish with fresh basil leaves, if desired.

Nutritional Information (per serving): Calories: 350 Protein: 18g Carbohydrates: 38g Fat: 14g Fiber: 2g Cholesterol: 40mg Sodium: 650mg Potassium: 200mg

Prosciutto e Funghi Pizza

Yield: 4 servings | Prep time: 25 minutes | Cook time: 15 minutes

Ingredients:

- 1 pizza dough
- 1/2 cup pizza sauce
- 1 cup mozzarella cheese
- Fresh basil leaves, for garnish (optional)
- 1/2 cup sliced mushrooms
- 4 slices prosciutto
- 1/4 cup grated Parmesan cheese

Directions:

1. Preheat oven to 450°F (230°C) with a pizza stone or baking sheet inside.
2. Roll out dough and transfer to a pizza peel or lined baking sheet.
3. Spread pizza sauce evenly over the dough. Sprinkle mozzarella cheese on top.
4. Arrange mushrooms and prosciutto pieces on the cheese.
5. Sprinkle grated Parmesan cheese over the toppings.
6. Transfer the pizza to the preheated oven.
7. Bake for 12-15 minutes until crust is golden and cheese is melted.
8. Let it cool slightly, then slice and serve.
9. Garnish with fresh basil leaves, if desired.

Nutritional Information (per serving): Calories: 380 Protein: 18g Carbohydrates: 42g Fat: 16g Fiber: 2g Cholesterol: 25mg Sodium: 760mg Potassium: 220mg

Diavola Pizza

Yield: 4 servings | Prep time: 20 minutes | Cook time: 15 minutes

Ingredients:

- 1 pizza dough
- 1/2 cup pizza sauce
- 1 cup mozzarella cheese
- 1/4 cup sliced pepperoni
- Fresh basil leaves, for garnish (optional)
- 2 tbsp sliced black olives
- 1/2 tsp dried oregano
- 1/4 tsp red pepper flakes

Directions:

1. Preheat oven to 450°F (230°C) with a pizza stone or baking sheet inside.
2. Roll out dough and transfer to a pizza peel or lined baking sheet.
3. Spread pizza sauce evenly over the dough.
4. Sprinkle mozzarella cheese on top.
5. Arrange pepperoni and black olives on the cheese.
6. Sprinkle dried oregano and red pepper flakes over the toppings.
7. Transfer the pizza to the preheated oven.
8. Bake for 12-15 minutes until crust is golden and cheese is melted.
9. Let it cool slightly, then slice and serve.
10. Garnish with fresh basil leaves, if desired.

Nutritional Information (per serving): Calories: 320 Protein: 14g Carbohydrates: 36g Fat: 14g Fiber: 2g Cholesterol: 30mg Sodium: 780mg Potassium: 180mg

Focaccia Bread
Yield: 6 servings | Prep time: 15 minutes | Cook time: 25 minutes

Ingredients:

- 2 1/4 cups all-purpose flour
- 1 tsp instant yeast
- 1 tsp salt
- 1 tsp sugar
- Coarse salt, for sprinkling
- 1 cup warm water
- 3 tbsp olive oil
- 1 tsp dried rosemary

Directions:

1. Combine flour, yeast, salt, and sugar in a bowl.
2. Gradually add warm water and olive oil, mixing until a soft dough forms.
3. Knead the dough on a floured surface for 5 minutes.
4. Let the dough rise in a greased bowl for 1 hour.
5. Preheat the oven to 425°F (220°C).
6. Transfer the dough to a greased baking sheet and press/stretch to fit.
7. Drizzle olive oil on top and sprinkle with rosemary and coarse salt.
8. Let it rest for 15 minutes.
9. Bake for 20-25 minutes until golden brown.
10. Cool, slice, and serve your delicious Focaccia Bread!

Nutritional Information (per serving): Calories: 230 Protein: 5g Carbohydrates: 39g Fat: 6g Fiber: 2g Cholesterol: 0mg Sodium: 390mg Potassium: 60mg

Arancini
Yield: 4 servings | Prep time: 30 minutes | Cook time: 25 minutes

Ingredients:

- 2 cups cooked risotto
- 4 oz mozzarella cheese, cubed
- 1/4 cup grated Parmesan cheese
- Marinara sauce, for serving
- 2 eggs
- 1 cup breadcrumbs
- Vegetable oil, for frying

Directions:

1. Flatten 2 tbsp of risotto in your hand, place a mozzarella cube in the center, and shape into a ball.
2. Repeat with the remaining risotto and cheese.
3. Dip each ball in beaten eggs, then roll in breadcrumbs.
4. Fry the rice balls in hot oil until golden brown and crispy.
5. Drain on paper towels.
6. Serve hot with marinara sauce.
7. Enjoy your tasty Arancini!

Nutritional Information (per serving): Calories: 290 Protein: 13g Carbohydrates: 29g Fat: 14g Fiber: 2g Cholesterol: 90mg Sodium: 530mg Potassium: 130mg

Bruschetta

Yield: 4 servings | Prep time: 10 minutes | Cook time: 5 minutes

Ingredients:

- 4 slices of crusty bread
- 2 large tomatoes, diced
- 2 cloves of garlic, minced
- Salt and pepper, to taste
- 1/4 cup fresh basil leaves, chopped
- 2 tbsp extra virgin olive oil
- 1 tbsp balsamic vinegar

Directions:

1. Toast bread slices in the oven at 400°F (200°C) for 5 minutes.
2. In a bowl, combine tomatoes, garlic, basil, olive oil, balsamic vinegar, salt, and pepper.
3. Rub garlic on one side of each bread slice.
4. Spread tomato mixture on the garlic-rubbed side of the bread.
5. Drizzle with extra olive oil and balsamic vinegar, if desired.
6. Serve immediately as an appetizer or snack.
7. Enjoy your delicious Bruschetta!

Nutritional Information (Per serving): Calories: 170 Protein: 4g Carbohydrates: 20g Fat: 9g Fiber: 2g Cholesterol: 0mg Sodium: 250mg Potassium: 290mg

Calzone

Yield: 4 servings | Prep time: 20 minutes | Cook time: 25 minutes

Ingredients:

- 1 lb pizza dough
- 1 cup marinara sauce
- 1 cup shredded mozzarella cheese
- 1/2 cup sliced pepperoni
- Olive oil
- Assorted vegetables (black olives, mushrooms, bell peppers, onions)
- 1/2 tsp dried oregano

Directions:

1. Preheat oven to 425°F (220°C).
2. Roll out pizza dough into 4 circles.
3. Spread marinara sauce on one half of each dough circle.
4. Top with mozzarella cheese, pepperoni, vegetables, and oregano.
5. Fold the dough over to form a half-moon shape and seal the edges.
6. Brush with olive oil.
7. Bake for 20-25 minutes until golden and crispy.
8. Let cool slightly before serving.
9. Enjoy your tasty Calzone!

Nutritional Information (per serving): Calories: 480 Protein: 22g Carbohydrates: 58g Fat: 18g Fiber: 4g Cholesterol: 35mg Sodium: 1180mg Potassium: 260mg

Panzerotti

Yield: 4 servings | Prep time: 30 minutes | Cook time: 15 minutes

Ingredients:

- 1 lb pizza dough
- 1 cup ricotta cheese
- 1 cup shredded mozzarella cheese
- 1/2 cup marinara sauce
- Vegetable oil
- 1/4 cup grated Parmesan cheese
- 1/4 cup chopped fresh basil
- 1/2 tsp dried oregano
- Salt and pepper

Directions:

1. Heat vegetable oil to 375°F (190°C).
2. Roll out pizza dough and cut into 4 pieces.
3. Mix ricotta, mozzarella, marinara sauce, Parmesan, basil, oregano, salt, and pepper.
4. Spoon cheese mixture onto half of each dough piece.
5. Fold dough over and seal edges with a fork.
6. Fry panzerotti until golden brown, 3-5 minutes per side.
7. Drain on paper towels.
8. Serve hot and enjoy your Panzerotti!

Nutritional Information (per serving): Calories: 420 Protein: 20g Carbohydrates: 43g Fat: 19g Fiber: 2g Cholesterol: 40mg Sodium: 580mg Potassium: 200mg

Suppli

Yield: 4 servings | Prep time: 25 minutes | Cook time: 20 minutes

Ingredients:

- 2 cups cooked risotto
- 1/2 cup diced mozzarella cheese
- 1/4 cup grated Parmesan cheese
- 1/4 cup chopped fresh parsley
- Salt and pepper
- 2 large eggs
- 1/2 cup all-purpose flour
- 1 cup breadcrumbs
- Vegetable oil

Directions:

1. Combine risotto, mozzarella, Parmesan, parsley, salt, and pepper.
2. Shape risotto mixture into small balls with an indentation.
3. Place mozzarella in the indentation and reshape the ball.
4. Roll in flour, dip in beaten eggs, and coat with breadcrumbs.
5. Heat vegetable oil to 375°F (190°C).
6. Fry suppli until golden brown and crispy, about 3-4 minutes.
7. Drain on paper towels.
8. Serve hot and enjoy your Suppli!

Nutritional Information (per serving): Calories: 320 Protein: 12g Carbohydrates: 38g Fat: 13g Fiber: 2g Cholesterol: 85mg Sodium: 360mg Potassium: 150mg

Polenta Fries

Yield: 4 servings | Prep time: 15 minutes | Cook time: 25 minutes

Ingredients:

- 1 cup instant polenta
- 4 cups water
- 1/2 cup grated Parmesan cheese
- 1/2 tsp garlic powder
- Marinara sauce
- 1/2 tsp paprika
- Salt and pepper
- Vegetable oil

Directions:

1. Cook polenta in boiling water, stirring until thickened.
2. Stir in Parmesan, garlic powder, paprika, salt, and pepper.
3. Spread polenta on a baking sheet and refrigerate for 1 hour.
4. Cut polenta into fry shapes.
5. Fry in oil at 375°F (190°C) until golden brown, about 3-4 minutes.
6. Drain on paper towels.
7. Serve hot with marinara sauce. Enjoy!

Nutritional Information (per serving): Calories: 220 Protein: 6g Carbohydrates: 40g Fat: 4g Fiber: 2g Cholesterol: 6mg Sodium: 300mg Potassium: 80mg

Crostini

Yield: 4 servings | Prep time: 10 minutes | Cook time: 10 minutes

Ingredients:

- Baguette or Italian bread
- Olive oil
- Garlic cloves
- Toppings of your choice

Directions:

1. Slice and toast bread.
2. Brush with olive oil.
3. Rub with garlic cloves.
4. Add toppings.
5. Bake until heated.
6. Serve and enjoy!

Nutritional Information (per serving): Calories: 120 Protein: 3g Carbohydrates: 20g Fat: 3g Fiber: 1g Cholesterol: 0mg Sodium: 160mg Potassium: 40mg

Olive Ascolane

Yield: 4 servings | Prep time: 30 minutes | Cook time: 15 minutes

Ingredients:

- 16 large green olives, pitted
- 1/2 cup ground beef
- 1/4 cup grated Parmesan cheese
- 2 tbsp bread crumbs
- Vegetable oil, for frying

- 1 egg, beaten
- 1/4 tsp salt
- 1/4 tsp black pepper

Directions:

1. Rinse the pitted olives under cold water and pat dry.
2. In a bowl, combine ground beef, Parmesan cheese, bread crumbs, beaten egg, salt, and black pepper.
3. Take a small amount of the beef mixture and stuff it into each olive.
4. Roll the stuffed olives in flour to coat lightly.
5. Heat vegetable oil in a deep fryer or skillet to 350°F (175°C).
6. Fry the stuffed olives until golden brown, about 3-4 minutes.
7. Remove from the oil and drain on paper towels.
8. Serve hot as an appetizer or snack.

Nutritional Information (per serving): Calories: 180 Protein: 9g Carbohydrates: 7g Fat: 13g Fiber: 2g Cholesterol: 65mg Sodium: 330mg Potassium: 140mg

Beans, Rice & Grains dishes

Risotto alla Milanese (Saffron Risotto)
Yield: 4 servings | Prep time: 10 minutes | Cook time: 25 minutes

Ingredients:

- 2 cups Arborio rice
- 4 cups vegetable or chicken broth
- 1/2 cup dry white wine
- 1/2 onion, finely chopped
- Salt and pepper to taste

- 2 tbsp butter
- 1/2 cup grated Parmesan cheese
- 1/4 tsp saffron threads

Directions:

1. Sauté onion in butter until translucent.
2. Add Arborio rice and cook until coated with butter. Pour in white wine and let it evaporate.
3. Gradually add broth, stirring until absorbed. Stir in saffron dissolved in water.
4. Continue adding broth until rice is creamy and al dente.
5. Remove from heat and stir in Parmesan cheese.
6. Season with salt and pepper.
7. Rest for a few minutes before serving.
8. Enjoy hot!

Nutritional Information (per serving): Calories: 350 Protein: 8g Carbohydrates: 70g Fat: 6g Fiber: 2g Cholesterol: 15mg Sodium: 800mg Potassium: 200mg

Pasta e Fagioli (Pasta with Beans)
Yield: 4 servings | Prep time: 10 minutes | Cook time: 30 minutes

Ingredients:

- 2 tbsp olive oil
- 1 onion, finely chopped
- 2 cloves garlic, minced
- 2 carrots, diced
- 2 celery stalks, diced
- 1 can diced tomatoes
- 4 cups vegetable broth

- 1 can cannellini beans, drained
- 1 cup ditalini pasta
- 1 tsp dried oregano
- 1 tsp dried basil
- Salt and pepper to taste
- Fresh parsley (for garnish)

Directions:

1. Sauté onion, garlic, carrots, and celery in olive oil.
2. Add diced tomatoes, vegetable broth, beans, oregano, and basil.
3. Season with salt and pepper. Simmer for 15 minutes.
4. Cook ditalini pasta separately. Add cooked pasta to the pot.
5. Simmer for 5 minutes. Adjust seasoning.
6. Serve hot, garnished with parsley.

Nutritional Information (per serving): Calories: 320 Protein: 10g Carbohydrates: 52g Fat: 8g Fiber: 10g Cholesterol: 0mg Sodium: 800mg Potassium: 600mg

Polenta e Funghi (Polenta with Mushrooms)

Yield: 4 servings | Prep time: 15 minutes | Cook time: 30 minutes

Ingredients:

- 1 cup polenta (cornmeal)
- 4 cups water
- 1 tsp salt
- 2 tbsp butter
- 1 lb mushrooms, sliced
- 2 cloves garlic, minced
- 1 tsp dried thyme
- Salt and pepper to taste
- Grated Parmesan cheese (for serving)
- Fresh parsley (for garnish)

Directions:

1. In a large pot, bring water to a boil.
2. Gradually whisk in the polenta and salt.
3. Reduce heat to low and cook, stirring constantly, for about 20-25 minutes until thickened.
4. Meanwhile, melt butter in a skillet over medium heat.
5. Add mushrooms, garlic, and dried thyme.
6. Sauté until mushrooms are golden brown and tender.
7. Season with salt and pepper.
8. Remove polenta from heat and stir in the sautéed mushrooms.
9. Serve hot, topped with grated Parmesan cheese and garnished with fresh parsley.

Nutritional Information (Per serving): Calories: 250 Protein: 6g Carbohydrates: 45g Fat: 6g Fiber: 6g Cholesterol: 10mg Sodium: 400mg Potassium: 350mg

Arancini di Riso (Rice Balls)

Yield: 12 servings | Prep time: 30 minutes | Cook time: 30 minutes

Ingredients:

- 2 cups cooked risotto rice
- 1/2 cup grated Parmesan cheese
- 2 eggs
- Marinara sauce (for serving)
- 1/2 cup breadcrumbs
- 12 small cubes of mozzarella cheese
- Vegetable oil (for frying)

Directions:

1. Mix cooked risotto rice, Parmesan cheese, and beaten eggs.
2. Shape rice mixture into balls, encasing a mozzarella cube inside each.
3. Coat balls in breadcrumbs.
4. Fry in hot oil until golden brown, about 4-5 minutes.
5. Drain excess oil on paper towels.
6. Serve hot with marinara sauce.

Nutritional Information (per serving): Calories: 180 Protein: 7g Carbohydrates: 22g Fat: 7g Fiber: 1g Cholesterol: 45mg Sodium: 300mg Potassium: 100mg

Farro Salad

Yield: 4 servings | Prep time: 10 minutes | Cook time: 20 minutes

Ingredients:

- 1 cup farro
- 2 cups water
- 1 cucumber, diced
- 1 bell pepper, diced
- 1/2 red onion, finely chopped
- 1/2 cup cherry tomatoes, halved
- 1/4 cup fresh parsley, chopped
- 1/4 cup feta cheese, crumbled
- 2 tablespoons lemon juice
- 2 tablespoons olive oil
- Salt and pepper to tast

Directions:

1. Rinse the farro under cold water.
2. In a saucepan, bring the water to a boil and add the farro.
3. Reduce heat, cover, and simmer for 20 minutes or until the farro is tender.
4. Drain any excess water and let the farro cool.
5. In a large bowl, combine the cooled farro, cucumber, bell pepper, red onion, cherry tomatoes, parsley, and feta cheese. In a small bowl, whisk together lemon juice, olive oil, salt, and pepper.
6. Pour the dressing over the salad and toss to combine.
7. Serve chilled or at room temperature.

Nutritional Information (per serving): Calories: 230 Protein: 6g Carbohydrates: 37g Fat: 7g Fiber: 6g Cholesterol: 5mg Sodium: 200mg Potassium: 270mg

Cannellini Bean Soup

Yield: 4 servings | Prep time: 10 minutes | Cook time: 30 minutes

Ingredients:

- 1 tbsp olive oil
- 1 onion, chopped
- 2 cloves garlic, minced
- 2 carrots, diced
- 2 celery stalks, diced
- Fresh parsley (optional)
- 2 cans cannellini beans, drained and rinsed
- 4 cups vegetable broth
- 1 bay leaf
- 1 tsp dried thyme
- Salt and pepper to taste

Directions:

1. Sauté onion and garlic in olive oil. Add carrots and celery, cook for 5 minutes.
2. Add beans, broth, bay leaf, and thyme. Bring to a boil, then simmer for 20 minutes.
3. Remove bay leaf.
4. Blend a portion of the soup until smooth.
5. Return to pot and stir.
6. Season with salt and pepper.
7. Simmer for 5 more minutes.
8. Serve hot, garnished with parsley.

Nutritional Information (per serving): Calories: 180 Protein: 8g Carbs: 32g Fat: 3g Fiber: 9g Cholesterol: 0mg Sodium: 600mg Potassium: 700mg

Parmigiano Reggiano Risotto

Yield: 4 servings | Prep time: 10 minutes | Cook time: 25 minutes

Ingredients:

- 1 ½ cups Arborio rice
- 4 cups vegetable broth
- 1 cup grated Parmigiano Reggiano cheese
- 1/2 cup dry white wine
- 1/4 cup unsalted butter
- Fresh parsley for garnish
- 1 small onion, finely chopped
- 2 cloves garlic, minced
- 2 tbsp olive oil
- Salt and pepper to taste

Directions:

1. Sauté onion and garlic in olive oil and 1 tbsp butter.
2. Add Arborio rice and cook for 2 minutes.
3. Pour in white wine and cook until absorbed.
4. Gradually add warm vegetable broth, stirring until absorbed.
5. Continue adding broth and stirring until rice is creamy and al dente (18-20 minutes).
6. Stir in grated Parmigiano Reggiano cheese and remaining butter.
7. Season with salt and pepper. Let it rest for a minute.
8. Garnish with parsley and serve.

Nutritional Information (per serving): Calories: 400 Protein: 12g Carbs: 55g Fat: 14g Fiber: 2g Cholesterol: 40mg Sodium: 800mg Potassium: 200mg

Ribollita (Tuscan Bean and Vegetable Soup)

Yield: 4 servings | Prep time: 15 minutes | Cook time: 1 hour

Ingredients:

- 2 cups cannellini beans, cooked
- 2 carrots, diced
- 2 celery stalks, diced
- 1 onion, chopped
- 3 garlic cloves, minced
- 1 bunch kale, chopped
- Grated Parmesan cheese for serving
- 1 can diced tomatoes
- 4 cups vegetable broth
- 2 tbsp olive oil
- 1 tsp dried thyme
- 1 tsp dried rosemary
- Salt and pepper to taste

Directions:

1. Heat olive oil in a large pot and sauté onion, garlic, carrots, and celery until softened.
2. Add kale, dried thyme, and dried rosemary. Cook until kale wilts.
3. Pour in diced tomatoes and vegetable broth. Bring to a boil.
4. Reduce heat and simmer for 30 minutes.
5. Add cooked cannellini beans and simmer for an additional 15 minutes.
6. Season with salt and pepper to taste. Ladle the soup into bowls and sprinkle with grated Parmesan cheese.
7. Serve hot.

Nutritional Information (per serving): Calories: 280 Protein: 12g Carbohydrates: 45g Fat: 6g Fiber: 12g Cholesterol: 0mg Sodium: 900mg Potassium: 800mg

Pasta e Ceci (Pasta with Chickpeas)

Yield: 4 servings | Prep time: 10 minutes | Cook time: 25 minutes

Ingredients:

- 8 oz pasta
- 1 can chickpeas, drained
- 2 cloves garlic, minced
- 1 small onion, chopped
- 2 tbsp olive oil
- Fresh parsley for garnish

- 1 can diced tomatoes
- 4 cups vegetable broth
- 1 tsp dried oregano
- Salt and pepper to taste

Directions:

1. Cook pasta, then set aside.
2. Sauté garlic and onion in olive oil.
3. Add tomatoes, chickpeas, broth, oregano, and optional red pepper flakes.
4. Simmer for 15 minutes.
5. Season with salt and pepper.
6. Add pasta and simmer 5 more minutes.
7. Serve hot, garnish with parsley.

Nutritional Information (per serving): Calories: 380 Protein: 15g Carbohydrates: 64g Fat: 8g Fiber: 12g Cholesterol: 0mg Sodium: 850mg Potassium: 450mg

Gnocchi alla Romana (Roman-Style Semolina Gnocchi)

Yield: 4 servings | Prep time: 30 minutes | Cook time: 30 minutes

Ingredients:

- 1 cup semolina flour
- 4 cups milk
- 1 cup grated Parmesan cheese
- Butter for greasing

- 2 large egg yolks
- Salt and pepper to taste

Directions:

1. Heat milk, whisk in semolina flour, and cook until thickened.
2. Remove from heat, cool slightly, and add Parmesan, egg yolks, salt, and pepper.
3. Transfer to greased baking dish and let cool completely.
4. Cut out individual gnocchi using a round cookie cutter.
5. Place on a buttered baking sheet and bake at 400°F (200°C) for 20 minutes.
6. Serve hot as a main course or side dish.

Nutritional Information (per serving): Calories: 380 Protein: 15g Carbohydrates: 50g Fat: 12g Fiber: 2g Cholesterol: 95mg Sodium: 520mg Potassium: 300mg.

Risi e Bisi (Rice and Peas)

Yield: 4 servings | Prep time: 10 minutes | Cook time: 30 minutes

Ingredients:

- 1 cup Arborio rice
- 2 cups fresh or frozen peas
- 4 cups vegetable or chicken broth
- 1 small onion, finely chopped
- Fresh parsley for garnish
- 2 tablespoons butter
- 1/4 cup grated Parmesan cheese
- Salt and pepper to taste

Directions:

1. In a large pot, melt the butter over medium heat and sauté the chopped onion until translucent.
2. Add the rice and cook for a couple of minutes, stirring constantly.
3. Pour in 1 cup of broth and stir until most of the liquid is absorbed.
4. Continue adding the broth, 1 cup at a time, stirring frequently, until the rice is cooked and creamy (about 20-25 minutes).
5. Stir in the peas and cook for an additional 5 minutes, or until the peas are tender.
6. Remove from heat and stir in the grated Parmesan cheese.
7. Season with salt and pepper to taste.
8. Serve hot, garnished with fresh parsley.

Nutritional Information (per serving): Calories: 280 Protein: 8g Carbohydrates: 51g Fat: 5g Fiber: 6g Cholesterol: 12mg Sodium: 760mg Potassium: 350mg.

Fagioli all'Uccelletto (Tuscan-style Beans)

Yield: 4 servings | Prep time: 10 minutes | Cook time: 40 minutes

Ingredients:

- 2 cups cannellini beans (cooked or canned)
- 2 tbsp olive oil
- 4 cloves garlic, minced
- 1 small onion, finely chopped
- Fresh parsley for garnish
- 1 can (14 oz) diced tomatoes
- 1/2 cup vegetable or chicken broth
- 1 tsp dried rosemary
- Salt and pepper to taste

Directions:

1. Sauté garlic and onion in olive oil until translucent.
2. Add tomatoes, cook briefly.
3. Mix in beans, broth, and rosemary.
4. Season with salt and pepper.
5. Simmer on low for 30 minutes.
6. Garnish with parsley and serve hot.

Nutritional Information (per serving): Calories: 220 Protein: 10g Carbohydrates: 35g Fat: 5g Fiber: 9g Cholesterol: 0mg Sodium: 480mg Potassium: 680mg.

Cacio e Pepe (Pasta with Cheese and Pepper)
Yield: 4 servings | Prep time: 5 minutes | Cook time: 15 minutes

Ingredients:

- 12 oz spaghetti or bucatini pasta
- 1 cup grated Pecorino Romano cheese
- Extra virgin olive oil (optional, for drizzling)
- 1 tsp freshly ground black pepper
- Salt to taste

Directions:

1. Cook pasta in salted boiling water until al dente.
2. In a separate pan, toast black pepper over low heat for a minute.
3. Reserve 1 cup of pasta water, then drain the cooked pasta.
4. Return the pasta to the pan and add half of the reserved pasta water.
5. Gradually sprinkle in the grated Pecorino Romano cheese while tossing the pasta.
6. Add more pasta water if needed to create a creamy sauce.
7. Season with salt to taste.
8. Serve immediately, drizzling with olive oil if desired.

Nutritional Information (per serving): Calories: 400 Protein: 16g Carbohydrates: 50g Fat: 14g Fiber: 3g Cholesterol: 35mg Sodium: 600mg Potassium: 150mg.

Orzo Salad with Vegetables
Yield: 4 servings | Prep time: 10 minutes | Cook time: 10 minutes

Ingredients:

- 1 cup orzo pasta
- 1 cup cherry tomatoes, halved
- 1 cup cucumber, diced
- 1/2 cup red onion, finely chopped
- 1/2 cup Kalamata olives, pitted and sliced
- Salt and pepper to taste
- 1/4 cup feta cheese, crumbled
- 2 tablespoons fresh parsley, chopped
- 2 tablespoons fresh lemon juice
- 3 tablespoons extra-virgin olive oil

Directions:

1. Cook orzo pasta according to package instructions. Drain and let it cool.
2. In a large bowl, combine the cooked orzo, cherry tomatoes, cucumber, red onion, olives, and feta cheese.
3. In a small bowl, whisk together the lemon juice, olive oil, salt, and pepper to make the dressing.
4. Pour the dressing over the orzo and vegetables, tossing gently to combine.
5. Sprinkle fresh parsley on top for added freshness and flavor.

Nutritional Information (per serving): Calories: 280 Protein: 6g Carbohydrates: 32g Fat: 15g Fiber: 3g Cholesterol: 5mg Sodium: 280mg Potassium: 220mg.

Lentil Soup
Yield: 4 servings | Prep time: 10 minutes | Cook time: 30 minutes

Ingredients:

- 1 cup dried lentils
- 1 onion, chopped
- 2 carrots, diced
- 2 celery stalks, diced
- 2 garlic cloves, minced
- Fresh parsley, for garnish
- 4 cups vegetable broth
- 1 bay leaf
- 1 teaspoon ground cumin
- 1 teaspoon paprika
- Salt and pepper to taste

Directions:

1. Rinse the lentils under cold water and set aside.
2. In a large pot, heat some oil over medium heat. Add the onion, carrots, celery, and garlic. Sauté until the vegetables are tender.
3. Add the lentils, vegetable broth, bay leaf, cumin, paprika, salt, and pepper to the pot. Stir well to combine.
4. Bring the mixture to a boil, then reduce the heat to low. Cover the pot and let it simmer for about 25-30 minutes or until the lentils are cooked and tender.
5. Remove the bay leaf from the soup. Taste and adjust the seasoning if needed.
6. Serve the lentil soup hot, garnished with fresh parsley.

Nutritional Information (per serving): Calories: 220 Protein: 14g Carbohydrates: 40g Fat: 1g Fiber: 15g Cholesterol: 0mg Sodium: 800mg Potassium: 980mg.

Fish & Seafood dishes

Branzino al Sale (Salt-Baked Sea Bass)
Yield: 4 servings | Prep time: 20 mins | Cook time: 40 mins

Ingredients:

- 2 branzino (1 lb each), gutted and scaled
- 4 lbs coarse sea salt
- 4 egg whites
- 2 lemons, thinly sliced
- Black pepper to taste
- 4 sprigs fresh thyme
- 2 sprigs fresh rosemary
- 1 tbsp olive oil

Directions:

1. Preheat oven to 400°F (200°C). Mix sea salt and egg whites in a bowl.
2. Stuff branzino with lemon slices, thyme, and rosemary.
3. Spread salt mixture on baking sheet. Place branzino on top and cover with remaining salt.
4. Bake for 35-40 mins until salt crust is golden brown.
5. Let it rest, then crack open the crust. Brush off excess salt.
6. Fillet and serve with olive oil and black pepper.

Nutritional Information (per serving): Calories: 260 Protein: 35g Carbs: 0g Fat: 12g Fiber: 0g Cholesterol: 90mg Sodium: 4000mg Potassium: 700mg

Spaghetti alle Vongole (Spaghetti with Clams)
Yield: 4 servings | Prep time: 10 mins | Cook time: 20 mins

Ingredients:

- 12 oz spaghetti
- 2 lbs fresh clams, scrubbed
- 4 tbsp olive oil
- 4 cloves garlic, minced
- Lemon wedges, for serving
- 1/2 tsp red pepper flakes (optional)
- 1/2 cup dry white wine
- 1/4 cup chopped fresh parsley
- Salt and black pepper to taste

Directions:

1. Cook spaghetti until al dente. Drain and set aside.
2. Heat olive oil in a skillet. Sauté garlic and red pepper flakes for 1 min.
3. Add clams and white wine. Cover and cook for 5-7 mins until clams open.
4. Remove unopened clams. Stir in spaghetti and parsley.
5. Season with salt and black pepper.
6. Serve with lemon wedges.

Nutritional Information (per serving): Calories: 420 Protein: 20g Carbs: 58g Fat: 12g Fiber: 3g Cholesterol: 30mg Sodium: 600mg Potassium: 450mg

Fritto Misto di Mare (Mixed Fried Seafood)
Yield: 4 servings | Prep time: 15 mins | Cook time: 10 mins

Ingredients:

- 1/2 lb shrimp, peeled and deveined
- 1/2 lb calamari rings
- 1/2 lb small fish fillets (such as smelts or whitebait)
- 1/2 cup all-purpose flour
- Lemon wedges, for serving
- 1/2 cup cornstarch
- 1 tsp salt
- 1/2 tsp paprika
- Vegetable oil, for frying

Directions:

1. Mix flour, cornstarch, salt, and paprika in a bowl.
2. Heat vegetable oil to 350°F (175°C) in a deep pan.
3. Coat seafood in the flour mixture, shaking off excess.
4. Fry seafood in batches until golden brown and crispy (2-3 mins per batch).
5. Drain on paper towels.
6. Serve with lemon wedges.

Nutritional Information (per serving): Calories: 350 Protein: 28g Carbs: 28g Fat: 14g Fiber: 1g Cholesterol: 180mg Sodium: 650mg Potassium: 380mg

Insalata di Mare (Seafood Salad)
Yield: 4 servings | Prep time: 20 mins | Cook time: 10 mins

Ingredients:

- 1/2 lb shrimp, peeled and deveined
- 1/2 lb calamari rings
- 1/2 lb mussels, cleaned and debearded
- 1/2 lb clams, scrubbed and rinsed
- 1/2 cup cherry tomatoes, halved
- Lemon wedges, for serving
- 1/4 cup red onion, thinly sliced
- 1/4 cup chopped fresh parsley
- 2 tbsp extra-virgin olive oil
- 1 tbsp lemon juice
- Salt and pepper to taste

Directions:

1. Cook shrimp, calamari, mussels, and clams separately until done. Let cool.
2. Cut shrimp into bite-sized pieces. Leave calamari, mussels, and clams whole or halved.
3. In a bowl, combine seafood, cherry tomatoes, red onion, and parsley.
4. Drizzle olive oil and lemon juice. Season with salt and pepper.
5. Gently toss to combine.
6. Cover and refrigerate for at least 1 hour.
7. Serve chilled with lemon wedges.

Nutritional Information (per serving): Calories: 220 Protein: 28g Carbs: 9g Fat: 8g Fiber: 1g Cholesterol: 150mg Sodium: 380mg Potassium: 380mg

Gamberi all'Aglio (Garlic Shrimp)

Yield: 4 servings | Prep time: 10 mins | Cook time: 10 mins

Ingredients:

- 1 lb large shrimp, peeled and deveined
- 4 tbsp olive oil
- 4 cloves garlic, minced
- 1/2 tsp red pepper flakes (optional)
- Lemon wedges, for serving
- 1 tbsp lemon juice
- 2 tbsp chopped fresh parsley
- Salt and pepper to taste

Directions:

1. Heat olive oil in a skillet over medium heat.
2. Sauté garlic and red pepper flakes for 1 min.
3. Add shrimp and cook for 2-3 mins per side until pink and opaque.
4. Drizzle with lemon juice and toss to coat.
5. Sprinkle with parsley, salt, and pepper.
6. Cook for 1 more min to meld flavors.
7. Serve hot with lemon wedges.

Nutritional Information (per serving): Calories: 220 Protein: 24g Carbs: 2g Fat: 13g Fiber: 0g Cholesterol: 190mg Sodium: 300mg Potassium: 220mg

Calamari Ripieni (Stuffed Calamari)

Yield: 4 servings | Prep time: 20 mins | Cook time: 30 mins

Ingredients:

- 8 small to medium-sized calamari tubes
- 1/2 cup breadcrumbs
- 1/4 cup grated Parmesan cheese
- 2 tbsp chopped fresh parsley
- 1 cup marinara sauce
- 2 cloves garlic, minced
- 2 tbsp olive oil
- 1/4 tsp dried oregano
- Salt and pepper to taste

Directions:

1. Preheat oven to 375°F (190°C).
2. Rinse calamari tubes and pat dry.
3. In a bowl, combine breadcrumbs, Parmesan, parsley, garlic, olive oil, oregano, salt, and pepper.
4. Stuff each calamari tube with breadcrumb mixture and secure openings with toothpicks.
5. Place stuffed calamari in a baking dish and pour marinara sauce over them.
6. Cover with foil and bake for 25 mins. Remove foil and bake for 5 more mins to brown tops.
7. Serve hot, garnished with additional parsley if desired.

Nutritional Information (per serving): Calories: 230 Protein: 22g Carbs: 15g Fat: 9g Fiber: 1g Cholesterol: 220mg Sodium: 520mg Potassium: 380mg

Zuppa di Pesce (Fish Soup)

Yield: 4 servings | Prep time: 15 mins | Cook time: 30 mins

Ingredients:

- 1 lb mixed fish fillets
- 1/2 lb shrimp
- 1/2 lb mussels
- 1/2 lb clams
- 2 tbsp olive oil
- 1 onion, chopped
- 2 cloves garlic, minced
- Fresh parsley, chopped, for garnish
- 1 can (14 oz) diced tomatoes
- 4 cups fish or vegetable broth
- 1/2 cup white wine
- 1 tsp dried basil
- 1 tsp dried oregano
- Salt and pepper to taste

Directions:

1. Heat olive oil in a pot over medium heat.
2. Sauté onion and garlic until softened.
3. Add diced tomatoes, broth, wine, basil, oregano, salt, and pepper. Bring to a boil.
4. Simmer for 15 mins.
5. Add fish, shrimp, mussels, and clams. Cover and cook for 10-12 mins until seafood is cooked and shells have opened.
6. Discard any unopened mussels or clams.
7. Ladle into bowls, garnish with parsley, and serve hot.

Nutritional Information (per serving): Calories: 280 Protein: 35g Carbs: 10g Fat: 10g Fiber: 2g Cholesterol: 150mg Sodium: 920mg Potassium: 750mg

Cozze alla Marinara (Mussels in Tomato Sauce)

Yield: 4 servings | Prep time: 10 mins | Cook time: 15 mins

Ingredients:

- 2 lbs fresh mussels
- 2 tbsp olive oil
- 4 cloves garlic, minced
- 1/2 tsp red pepper flakes
- Crusty bread, for serving
- 1 cup tomato sauce
- 1/2 cup white wine
- 2 tbsp chopped parsley
- Salt and pepper to taste

Directions:

1. Rinse mussels and discard cracked shells or unopened ones.
2. Heat olive oil in a pot over medium heat. Sauté garlic and red pepper flakes for 1 min.
3. Add tomato sauce and white wine, simmer.
4. Add mussels, cover, and cook for 5-7 mins until opened.
5. Discard unopened mussels.
6. Stir in parsley, season with salt and pepper.
7. Serve hot in bowls with cooking liquid and crusty bread.

Nutritional Information (per serving): Calories: 250 Protein: 20g Carbs: 10g Fat: 10g Fiber: 2g Cholesterol: 30mg Sodium: 700mg Potassium: 550mg

Grigliata di Pesce (Grilled Seafood)
Yield: 4 servings | Prep time: 20 mins | Cook time: 10 mins

Ingredients:

- 1 lb shrimp
- 1 lb calamari
- 1 lb fish fillets
- 2 tbsp olive oil
- 2 cloves garlic, minced
- Fresh parsley, chopped, for garnish
- 1 tbsp lemon juice
- 1 tsp dried oregano
- Salt and pepper to taste
- Lemon wedges, for serving

Directions:

1. Preheat grill to medium-high heat.
2. In a bowl, combine olive oil, minced garlic, lemon juice, dried oregano, salt, and pepper to make a marinade.
3. Toss shrimp, calamari, and fish in the marinade.
4. Thread seafood onto skewers.
5. Grill skewers for 4-5 mins per side until cooked and lightly charred.
6. Remove from grill and let rest.
7. Serve hot, garnished with parsley and accompanied by lemon wedges.

Nutritional Information (per serving): Calories: 320 Protein: 40g Carbs: 3g Fat: 16g Fiber: 1g Cholesterol: 240mg Sodium: 400mg Potassium: 550mg

Tonno alla Griglia (Grilled Tuna)
Yield: 4 servings | Prep time: 10 minutes | Cook time: 6 minutes

Ingredients:

- 1 lb fresh tuna steaks
- 2 tablespoons olive oil
- 2 cloves garlic, minced
- 1 tablespoon lemon juice
- Fresh parsley, chopped, for garnish
- 1 teaspoon dried oregano
- Salt and pepper to taste
- Lemon wedges, for serving

Directions:

1. Preheat the grill to medium-high heat.
2. Rub the tuna steaks with olive oil, minced garlic, lemon juice, dried oregano, salt, and pepper.
3. Place the tuna steaks on the grill and cook for about 3 minutes per side for medium-rare, or adjust the cooking time to your desired level of doneness.
4. Remove the tuna steaks from the grill and let them rest for a couple of minutes.
5. Slice the grilled tuna steaks into thin slices.
6. Serve the Tonno alla Griglia hot, garnished with fresh parsley and accompanied by lemon wedges.

Nutritional Information (per serving): Calories: 250 Protein: 35g Carbohydrates: 1g Fat: 12g Fiber: 0g Cholesterol: 60mg Sodium: 350mg Potassium: 550mg

Risotto ai Frutti di Mare (Seafood Risotto)

Yield: 4 servings | Prep time: 10 mins | Cook time: 25 mins

Ingredients:

- 1 cup Arborio rice
- 1 lb mixed seafood
- 2 tbsp olive oil
- 1 onion, finely chopped
- 2 cloves garlic, minced
- Salt and pepper to taste

- 1/2 cup dry white wine
- 4 cups seafood or vegetable broth
- 1/2 cup grated Parmesan cheese
- 2 tbsp butter
- Fresh parsley, chopped, for garnish

Directions:

1. Sauté onion and garlic in olive oil.
2. Add rice and cook until translucent.
3. Pour in white wine and cook until evaporated.
4. Gradually add broth, stirring until absorbed.
5. Cook mixed seafood separately and set aside.
6. Remove risotto from heat, stir in Parmesan and butter.
7. Season with salt and pepper.
8. Gently fold in cooked seafood.
9. Serve hot, garnished with parsley.

Nutritional Information (per serving): Calories: 420 Protein: 25g Carbs: 50g Fat: 12g Fiber: 2g Cholesterol: 75mg Sodium: 800mg Potassium: 450mg

Baccalà alla Livornese (Livorno-Style Salted Cod)

Yield: 4 servings | Prep time: 30 mins | Cook time: 30 mins

Ingredients:

- 1 lb salted cod fillets
- 2 tbsp olive oil
- 1 onion, chopped
- 2 cloves garlic, minced
- Salt and pepper to taste

- 1 can (14 oz) diced tomatoes
- 1/2 cup black olives, sliced
- 2 tbsp capers
- 1/4 cup fresh parsley, chopped

Directions:

1. Soak cod in water for 24 hours, drain, and rinse.
2. Sauté onion and garlic in olive oil.
3. Add tomatoes and simmer for 5 mins.
4. Cut cod into pieces and add to skillet. Cook for 10 mins.
5. Stir in olives, capers, and parsley. Season with salt and pepper.
6. Cook for 5 more mins.
7. Serve hot, garnished with parsley.

Nutritional Information (per serving): Calories: 220 Protein: 30g Carbs: 10g Fat: 7g Fiber: 2g Cholesterol: 60mg Sodium: 1300mg Potassium: 600mg

Salmone al Forno (Baked Salmon)

Yield: 4 servings | Prep time: 10 minutes | Cook time: 15 minutes

Ingredients:

- 4 salmon fillets (6 oz each)
- 2 tbsp olive oil
- 2 cloves garlic, minced
- 1 tsp lemon zest
- Fresh dill for garnish
- 1 tbsp fresh lemon juice
- 1 tsp dried dill
- Salt and pepper to taste
- Lemon slices for garnish

Directions:

1. Preheat the oven to 400°F (200°C) and line a baking sheet with parchment paper.
2. Place the salmon fillets on the prepared baking sheet.
3. In a small bowl, mix together olive oil, minced garlic, lemon zest, lemon juice, dried dill, salt, and pepper.
4. Drizzle the olive oil mixture over the salmon fillets, coating them evenly.
5. Bake the salmon in the preheated oven for 12-15 minutes, or until the fish is cooked through and flakes easily with a fork.
6. Remove the salmon from the oven and let it rest for a few minutes.
7. Garnish with lemon slices and fresh dill before serving.

Nutritional Information (per serving): Calories: 350 Protein: 34g Carbohydrates: 0g Fat: 24g Fiber: 0g Cholesterol: 95mg Sodium: 80mg Potassium: 740mg

Scampi all'Acqua Pazza (Scampi in Crazy Water)

Yield: 4 servings | Prep time: 15 minutes | Cook time: 20 minutes

Ingredients:

- 1 lb scampi (langoustines or large shrimp), cleaned and deveined
- 2 tbsp olive oil
- 2 cloves garlic, minced
- 1/2 cup cherry tomatoes, halved
- Red pepper flakes (optional)
- 1/4 cup white wine
- 1/4 cup fish broth or clam juice
- 1/4 cup fresh parsley, chopped
- Salt and pepper to taste

Directions:

1. Heat olive oil in a large skillet over medium heat.
2. Add minced garlic and sauté for 1 minute until fragrant.
3. Add scampi to the skillet and cook for 2 minutes on each side until they turn pink.
4. Add cherry tomatoes, white wine, and fish broth to the skillet. Season with salt, pepper, and red pepper flakes if desired.
5. Simmer for 10 minutes, allowing the flavors to meld together and the liquid to reduce slightly.
6. Stir in chopped parsley and cook for an additional 2 minutes.
7. Serve the scampi in a shallow bowl with the flavorful broth. Garnish with fresh parsley.

Nutritional Information (per serving): Calories: 220 Protein: 20g Carbohydrates: 5g Fat: 12g Fiber: 1g Cholesterol: 150mg Sodium: 280mg Potassium: 350mg

Alici Marinate (Marinated Anchovies)

Yield: 4 servings | Prep time: 15 minutes | Cook time: 0 minutes

Ingredients:

- 1 lb fresh anchovies, cleaned and deboned
- 1/4 cup extra-virgin olive oil
- 2 cloves garlic, minced
- Salt and pepper to taste
- 2 tbsp lemon juice
- 2 tbsp fresh parsley, chopped

Directions:

1. Rinse the anchovies under cold water and pat them dry with a paper towel.
2. In a bowl, combine olive oil, minced garlic, lemon juice, and chopped parsley. Season with salt and pepper.
3. Add the anchovies to the marinade and gently toss to coat them evenly. Ensure each anchovy is well covered in the marinade.
4. Cover the bowl with plastic wrap and refrigerate for at least 1 hour to allow the flavors to develop.
5. Serve the marinated anchovies as an appetizer or as part of an antipasto platter. They can be enjoyed on their own or served with crusty bread.

Nutritional Information (per serving): Calories: 180 Protein: 22g Carbohydrates: 2g Fat: 9g Fiber: 0g Cholesterol: 40mg Sodium: 260mg Potassium: 400mg

Poultry & Meat dishes.

Pollo alla Cacciatora (Hunter's Chicken)
Yield: 4 servings Prep time: 15 min Cook time: 1 hour

Ingredients:

- 4 chicken thighs
- 4 chicken drumsticks
- 2 tbsp olive oil
- 1 onion, diced
- 2 cloves garlic, minced
- 1 red bell pepper, sliced
- Fresh parsley for garnish

- 1 can diced tomatoes (400g)
- 1/2 cup chicken broth
- 1/2 cup red wine
- 1 tsp dried oregano
- 1 tsp dried basil
- Salt and pepper to taste

Directions:

1. Season chicken with salt and pepper.
2. Brown chicken in olive oil.
3. Sauté onion, garlic, and bell pepper.
4. Add tomatoes, broth, wine, oregano, and basil.
5. Return chicken to skillet and simmer covered for 45 min to 1 hour.
6. Adjust seasoning.
7. Serve hot, garnished with parsley.

Nutritional Information (per serving): Calories: 350 Protein: 28g Carbs: 10g Fat: 20g Fiber: 3g Cholesterol: 110mg Sodium: 450mg Potassium: 620mg.

Osso Buco (Braised Veal Shanks)
Yield: 4 servings Prep time: 20 min Cook time: 2 hours

Ingredients:

- 4 veal shanks
- Salt and pepper
- Flour
- 2 tbsp olive oil
- 1 onion, diced
- 2 carrots, diced
- 2 celery stalks, diced

- 4 garlic cloves, minced
- 1 cup white wine
- 1 can diced tomatoes (400g)
- 1 cup beef broth
- 2 bay leaves
- 1 tsp dried thyme
- Gremolata (parsley, garlic, lemon zest)

Directions:

1. Season veal shanks, dredge in flour. Brown shanks in olive oil, remove.
2. Sauté onion, carrots, celery, garlic.
3. Add wine, tomatoes, broth, bay leaves, thyme. Stir.
4. Return shanks, cover, simmer 2 hours.
5. Adjust seasoning.
6. Serve hot, garnish with gremolata.

Nutritional Information (per serving): Calories: 400 Protein: 30g Carbs: 10g Fat: 25g Fiber: 2g Cholesterol: 120mg Sodium: 600mg Potassium: 800mg.

Bistecca alla Fiorentina (Florentine Steak)
Yield: 2-6 servings Prep time: 5 min Cook time: 10-15 min

Ingredients:

- 1 large T-bone or Porterhouse steak (2-3 pounds)
- Salt
- Black pepper
- Olive oil
- Rosemary sprigs

Directions:

1. Preheat grill or broiler.
2. Season steak generously with salt and pepper.
3. Drizzle olive oil on both sides of the steak.
4. Grill or broil steak on high heat for 5-7 minutes per side (for medium-rare).
5. Allow the steak to rest for a few minutes.
6. Slice the steak across the grain into thick slices.
7. Serve hot, garnished with fresh rosemary sprigs.

Nutritional Information (per serving): Calories: 450 Protein: 50g Carbohydrates: 0g Fat: 30g Fiber: 0g Cholesterol: 150mg Sodium: 500mg Potassium: 700mg.

Vitello Tonnato (Veal with Tuna Sauce)
Yield: 4-6 servings Prep time: 15 min Cook time: 1 hour

Ingredients:

- lbs veal roast
- Salt, pepper
- 1 cup broth
- 1/4 cup white wine
- 1/2 cup mayonnaise
- Fresh parsley
- 1/4 cup canned tuna
- 2 anchovy fillets
- 2 tbsp capers
- Lemon juice

Directions:

1. Season veal with salt and pepper.
2. Roast veal in a covered pan with broth and wine at 325°F for 1 hour.
3. Slice veal and let it cool.
4. Blend mayonnaise, tuna, anchovies, and capers.
5. Season tuna sauce with lemon juice and salt.
6. Arrange veal slices, pour sauce over them, and garnish with parsley.
7. Refrigerate for 2 hours before serving.

Nutritional Information (per serving): Calories: 350 Protein: 28g Carbs: 2g Fat: 25g Fiber: 0.5g Cholesterol: 110mg Sodium: 450mg Potassium: 450mg.

Cotoletta alla Milanese (Milanese-Style Breaded Veal Cutlet)

Yield: 4 servings Prep time: 15 mins Cook time: 10 mins

Ingredients:

- 4 veal cutlets
- Salt, pepper
- Lemon wedges
- Flour, eggs, breadcrumbs
- Vegetable oil

Directions:

1. Season and coat cutlets.
2. Fry in oil until golden and cooked.
3. Drain on paper towels.
4. Serve with lemon wedges.

Nutritional Information (per serving): Calories: 400 Protein: 30g Carbs: 15g Fat: 24g Fiber: 1g Cholesterol: 160mg Sodium: 450mg Potassium: 500mg.

Arrosto di Maiale (Roast Pork)

Yield: 4 servings Prep time: 15 mins Cook time: 1 hour 30 mins

Ingredients:

- 2 lbs pork roast
- Salt, pepper
- Garlic, rosemary
- Olive oil

Directions:

1. Season pork with salt and pepper.
2. Insert garlic and rosemary into incisions.
3. Sear the roast in hot oil.
4. Roast in 350°F oven for 1 hr 30 mins.
5. Rest for 10 mins, then slice.

Nutritional Information (per serving): Calories: 350 Protein: 30g Carbs: 0g Fat: 25g Fiber: 0g Cholesterol: 90mg Sodium: 400mg Potassium: 500mg.

Pollo Marsala (Chicken Marsala)
Yield: 4 servings Prep time: 10 mins Cook time: 25 mins

Ingredients:

- 4 boneless, skinless chicken breasts
- Flour, salt, pepper
- Butter
- Fresh parsley

- Mushrooms
- Marsala wine
- Chicken broth

Directions:

1. Season and flour the chicken.
2. Brown the chicken in butter.
3. Sauté mushrooms, then add wine and broth.
4. Return chicken to the skillet and simmer.
5. Garnish with parsley.

Nutritional Information (per serving): Calories: 350 Protein: 30g Carbs: 10g Fat: 18g Fiber: 1g Cholesterol: 100mg Sodium: 400mg Potassium: 500mg.

Saltimbocca alla Romana (Roman-Style Veal)
Yield: 4 servings Prep time: 15 mins Cook time: 15 mins

Ingredients:

- 4 veal scaloppine
- Salt and pepper
- 8 sage leaves
- White wine

- 4 slices prosciutto
- Flour
- Butter

Directions:

1. Season veal with salt and pepper.
2. Place sage leaf on each veal slice, wrap with prosciutto.
3. Dredge veal in flour, shaking off excess.
4. Melt butter in skillet over medium heat.
5. Cook veal until browned on both sides.
6. Pour in white wine, simmer briefly.
7. Serve hot, garnish with sage leaves.

Nutritional Information (per serving): Calories: 300 Protein: 25g Carbs: 5g Fat: 18g Fiber: 1g Cholesterol: 80mg Sodium: 600mg Potassium: 400mg.

Scaloppine al Limone (Lemon Veal Scaloppine)

Yield: 4 servings Prep time: 10 mins Cook time: 10 mins

Ingredients:

- 4 veal scaloppine
- Salt and pepper
- Flour
- 2 tbsp butter
- Fresh parsley (for garnish)

- 1/4 cup lemon juice
- 1/4 cup chicken broth
- 2 tbsp capers

Directions:

1. Season and flour veal.
2. Sauté veal in butter until browned.
3. Add lemon juice, broth, and capers. Cook briefly.
4. Return veal to skillet. Cook until sauce thickens.
5. Serve hot, garnished with parsley.

Nutritional Information (per serving): Calories: 250 Protein: 30g Carbs: 4g Fat: 12g Fiber: 1g Cholesterol: 100mg Sodium: 400mg Potassium: 350mg.

Polpette di Carne (Italian Meatballs)

Yield: 4 servings Prep time: 20 mins Cook time: 25 mins

Ingredients:

- 1 lb ground beef
- 1/2 cup breadcrumbs
- 1/4 cup grated Parmesan cheese
- 1/4 cup chopped parsley
- 1/4 cup milk
- 2 cups marinara sauce

- 1 egg
- 2 cloves garlic, minced
- 1/2 tsp salt
- 1/4 tsp black pepper

Directions:

1. In a bowl, combine ground beef, breadcrumbs, Parmesan cheese, parsley, milk, egg, garlic, salt, and black pepper. Mix well.
2. Shape the mixture into small meatballs, about 1 inch in diameter.
3. Heat a skillet over medium heat and add the meatballs. Cook until browned on all sides.
4. Pour the marinara sauce over the meatballs and bring to a simmer.
5. Cover and cook for 15 minutes, or until the meatballs are cooked through.
6. Serve the meatballs with the marinara sauce. Enjoy!

Nutritional Information (per serving): Calories: 350 Protein: 25g Carbohydrates: 15g Fat: 20g Fiber: 2g Cholesterol: 100mg Sodium: 900mg Potassium: 450mg.

Spezzatino di Manzo (Beef Stew)
Yield: 4 servings Prep time: 15 mins Cook time: 2 hours

Ingredients:

- lbs beef stew meat
- 2 tbsp olive oil
- 1 onion, chopped
- 2 carrots, sliced
- 2 celery stalks, sliced
- 3 cloves garlic, minced
- Chopped parsley for garnish

- 2 tbsp tomato paste
- 2 cups beef broth
- 1 cup red wine
- 1 bay leaf
- 1 tsp dried thyme
- Salt and pepper to taste

Directions:

1. Brown beef in olive oil, set aside.
2. Sauté onion, carrots, celery, and garlic.
3. Stir in tomato paste.
4. Return beef to pot, add broth, wine, bay leaf, thyme, salt, and pepper.
5. Simmer covered for 1.5-2 hours.
6. Remove bay leaf and adjust seasoning.
7. Serve hot, garnished with parsley.

Nutritional Information (per serving): Calories: 400 Protein: 30g Carbs: 10g Fat: 25g Fiber: 2g Cholesterol: 90mg Sodium: 800mg Potassium: 700mg.

Fegato alla Veneziana (Venetian-Style Liver and Onions)
Yield: 4 servings Prep time: 10 minutes Cook time: 20 minutes

Ingredients:

- 1 lb calf liver
- 2 onions
- 4 tbsp butter
- Chopped parsley

- 2 tbsp olive oil
- Salt and pepper
- 1/4 cup white wine

Directions:

1. Cook onions in butter and olive oil until golden.
2. Season liver with salt and pepper.
3. Cook liver in the same skillet for 2 minutes per side.
4. Remove liver, deglaze with white wine.
5. Return liver and onions to the skillet, simmer for 2 minutes.
6. Serve hot, garnished with parsley.

Nutritional Information (per serving): Calories: 250 Protein: 25g Carbs: 10g Fat: 12g Fiber: 2g Cholesterol: 200mg Sodium: 300mg Potassium: 500mg.

Coniglio alla Cacciatora (Hunter's Rabbit)
Yield: 4 servings Prep time: 15 min Cook time: 1 hr 30 min

Ingredients:

- 1 rabbit
- 2 onions
- 3 cloves garlic
- 4 tomatoes
- 1 cup red wine
- Olive oil

- 1 cup chicken broth
- 1 tbsp tomato paste
- Rosemary and thyme sprigs
- Salt and pepper

Directions:

1. Season and brown rabbit.
2. Sauté onions and garlic.
3. Add tomatoes, wine, broth, and paste.
4. Return rabbit, add herbs.
5. Simmer covered for 1 hr.
6. Uncover, simmer 30 min.
7. Serve hot.

Nutritional Information (per serving): Calories: 350 Protein: 35g Carbs: 10g Fat: 15g Fiber: 2g Cholesterol: 100mg Sodium: 500mg Potassium: 600mg.

Agnello Scottadito (Grilled Lamb Chops)
Yield: 4 servings Prep time: 10 min Cook time: 12 min

Ingredients:

- 8 lamb chops
- Garlic
- Salt and pepper

- Rosemary
- Olive oil

Directions:

1. Season lamb chops and rub with garlic, rosemary, and olive oil.
2. Grill for 6 minutes per side.
3. Let rest and serve hot.

Nutritional Information (per serving): Calories: 350 Protein: 30g Carbs: 0g Fat: 25g Fiber: 0g Cholesterol: 100mg Sodium: 200mg Potassium: 400mg.

Porchetta (Roast Pork Loin with Herbs and Spices)
Yield: 4 servings Prep time: 20 min Cook time: 2 hours

Ingredients:

- 2 lbs pork loin
- Garlic, fennel seeds, rosemary, sage
- Olive oil
- Salt, black pepper

Directions:

1. Preheat oven to 325°F (165°C).
2. Make a paste with garlic, fennel seeds, rosemary, sage, salt, and pepper.
3. Spread the paste inside the butterflied pork loin.
4. Roll and tie the pork loin.
5. Rub with olive oil, salt, and pepper.
6. Roast for 2 hours at 325°F (165°C).
7. Rest for 10 minutes before slicing.

Nutritional Information (per serving): Calories: 300 Protein: 30g Carbs: 2g Fat: 18g Fiber: 1g Cholesterol: 90mg Sodium: 600mg Potassium: 450mg.

Vegetarian dishes

Caprese Salad

Yield: 2-6 servings | Prep time: 10 minutes | Cook time: 0 minutes

Ingredients:

- 2 large ripe tomatoes
- 8 ounces fresh mozzarella cheese
- 1 bunch fresh basil leaves
- Salt and pepper to taste
- 3 tablespoons extra virgin olive oil
- 2 tablespoons balsamic vinegar

Directions:

1. Slice the tomatoes and mozzarella cheese into 1/4-inch thick slices.
2. Arrange the tomato and mozzarella slices on a serving platter, alternating between them.
3. Place a basil leaf on top of each tomato and mozzarella slice.
4. Drizzle the olive oil and balsamic vinegar over the salad.
5. Season with salt and pepper to taste.
6. Let the salad sit for a few minutes to allow the flavors to meld together.
7. Serve and enjoy!

Nutritional Information (per serving): Calories: 180 Protein: 12g Carbohydrates: 4g Fat: 14g Fiber: 1g Cholesterol: 35mg Sodium: 180mg Potassium: 200mg

Margherita Pizza

Yield: 2-6 servings | Prep time: 15 minutes | Cook time: 15 minutes

Ingredients:

- 1 lb pizza dough
- 2 large tomatoes, sliced
- 8 oz fresh mozzarella cheese, sliced
- Salt and pepper to taste
- Fresh basil leaves
- 2 tbsp extra virgin olive oil
- 2 cloves garlic, minced

Directions:

1. Preheat oven to 475°F (245°C) and grease a baking sheet.
2. Roll out pizza dough on a floured surface and transfer to the baking sheet.
3. Mix olive oil and minced garlic in a small bowl, then brush it over the dough.
4. Arrange tomato and mozzarella slices on top of the dough.
5. Sprinkle torn basil leaves over the pizza.
6. Season with salt and pepper.
7. Bake for about 15 minutes until crust is golden and cheese is melted.
8. Let it cool for a few minutes, then slice and serve hot.

Nutritional Information (per serving): Calories: 280 Protein: 12g Carbohydrates: 32g Fat: 12g Fiber: 2g Cholesterol: 20mg Sodium: 400mg Potassium: 250mg

Eggplant Parmesan

Yield: 2-6 servings | Prep time: 20 minutes | Cook time: 40 minutes

Ingredients:

- 2 large eggplants
- 1 cup all-purpose flour
- 3 large eggs, beaten
- 2 cups breadcrumbs
- 1/2 cup grated Parmesan cheese
- Olive oil for frying

- 2 cups marinara sauce
- 2 cups shredded mozzarella cheese
- Fresh basil leaves
- Salt and pepper to taste

Directions:

1. Preheat oven to 375°F (190°C) and grease a baking dish.
2. Slice and salt eggplants, then pat them dry.
3. Set up a breading station with flour, beaten eggs, and breadcrumb mixture.
4. Dip eggplant slices in flour, then eggs, and coat with breadcrumbs.
5. Fry eggplant slices in olive oil until golden brown, then drain on paper towels.
6. Layer marinara sauce, eggplant slices, mozzarella, and basil in the baking dish.
7. Repeat layers, ending with mozzarella on top.
8. Bake for 30-35 minutes until cheese is melted and bubbly.
9. Let it cool briefly, then serve hot.

Nutritional Information (per serving): Calories: 360 Protein: 17g Carbohydrates: 45g Fat: 12g Fiber: 9g Cholesterol: 70mg Sodium: 1100mg Potassium: 950mg

Risotto Primavera

Yield: 2-6 servings | Prep time: 10 minutes | Cook time: 30 minutes

Ingredients:

- 2 tbsp olive oil
- 1 small onion, finely chopped
- 2 cloves garlic, minced
- 1 cup Arborio rice
- 1/2 cup white wine (optional)
- 4 cups vegetable broth
- Salt and pepper to taste

- 1 cup asparagus, trimmed and cut into 1-inch pieces
- 1 cup peas (fresh or frozen)
- 1 cup cherry tomatoes, halved
- 1/2 cup grated Parmesan cheese
- Fresh basil leaves, for garnish

Directions:

1. Sauté onion and garlic in olive oil until translucent. Add Arborio rice and cook for 2 minutes.
2. Optionally, add white wine and stir until absorbed.
3. Gradually add vegetable broth, stirring until absorbed before each addition.
4. Stir in asparagus, peas, and cherry tomatoes halfway through.
5. Continue adding broth until rice is creamy and al dente. Stir in Parmesan cheese, salt, and pepper.
6. Let it rest briefly, then serve garnished with basil.

Nutritional Information (per serving): Calories: 320 Protein: 9g Carbohydrates: 48g Fat: 9g Fiber: 5g Cholesterol: 10mg Sodium: 850mg Potassium: 420mg

Bruschetta

Yield: 2-6 servings | Prep time: 10 minutes | Cook time: 5 minutes

Ingredients:

- 6 slices of crusty Italian bread
- 2 large ripe tomatoes, diced
- 1/4 cup fresh basil leaves, chopped
- Salt and pepper to taste
- 2 cloves garlic, minced
- 2 tablespoons extra virgin olive oil
- 1 tablespoon balsamic vinegar

Directions:

1. Preheat the broiler on high.
2. Place the bread slices on a baking sheet and toast them under the broiler until golden brown on both sides.
3. In a bowl, combine the diced tomatoes, chopped basil, minced garlic, olive oil, balsamic vinegar, salt, and pepper. Mix well.
4. Remove the toasted bread from the oven and rub one side of each slice with a garlic clove.
5. Spoon the tomato mixture onto the garlic-rubbed side of each bread slice.
6. Drizzle with additional olive oil and balsamic vinegar if desired.
7. Serve the bruschetta immediately as an appetizer or light meal.

Nutritional Information (per serving): Calories: 180 Protein: 5g Carbohydrates: 26g Fat: 7g Fiber: 3g Cholesterol: 0mg Sodium: 240mg Potassium: 260mg

Pasta alla Norma

Yield: 2-6 servings | Prep time: 10 minutes | Cook time: 20 minutes

Ingredients:

- 8 oz pasta
- 2 large eggplants
- 4 tbsp olive oil
- 4 cloves garlic, minced
- 1 can (14 oz) diced tomatoes
- Fresh basil leaves, for garnish
- 1/2 tsp dried oregano
- 1/4 tsp red pepper flakes (optional)
- Salt and pepper to taste
- 1/4 cup grated ricotta salata or Parmesan cheese

Directions:

1. Cook pasta until al dente, then drain.
2. Slice and salt eggplants, then pat them dry.
3. Fry eggplant slices in olive oil until golden brown.
4. Sauté minced garlic in olive oil, then add tomatoes, oregano, red pepper flakes, salt, and pepper. Simmer for 10 minutes.
5. Add cooked eggplant slices to the sauce and cook for 5 more minutes.
6. Toss cooked pasta with eggplant and tomato sauce.
7. Serve garnished with grated cheese and fresh basil leaves.

Nutritional Information (per serving): Calories: 350 Protein: 10g Carbohydrates: 50g Fat: 14g Fiber: 8g Cholesterol: 5mg Sodium: 420mg Potassium: 650mg

Caponata

Yield: 2-6 servings | Prep time: 15 minutes | Cook time: 30 minutes

Ingredients:

- 2 eggplants, diced
- 1 onion, diced
- 2 celery stalks, diced
- 1 red bell pepper, diced
- 3 tbsp olive oil
- 2 cloves garlic, minced
- Salt and pepper to taste
- Fresh basil leaves, for garnish
- 1 can (14 oz) diced tomatoes
- 2 tbsp red wine vinegar
- 1 tbsp capers, drained
- 1/4 cup green olives, sliced
- 1 tbsp sugar

Directions:

1. Sauté eggplants, onion, celery, and red bell pepper in olive oil until tender.
2. Add minced garlic and cook for 1 minute.
3. Stir in diced tomatoes, red wine vinegar, capers, green olives, sugar, salt, and pepper.
4. Simmer covered for 20 minutes.
5. Serve warm or at room temperature, garnished with basil leaves.

Nutritional Information (per serving): Calories: 180 Protein: 3g Carbohydrates: 20g Fat: 11g Fiber: 7g Cholesterol: 0mg Sodium: 400mg Potassium: 650mg

Pesto Pasta

Yield: 2-6 servings | Prep time: 10 minutes | Cook time: 15 minutes

Ingredients:

- 8 ounces pasta (such as spaghetti or penne)
- 2 cups fresh basil leaves
- 1/2 cup grated Parmesan cheese
- 1/4 cup pine nuts
- Fresh basil leaves, for garnish
- 2 cloves garlic
- 1/2 cup extra virgin olive oil
- Salt and pepper to taste
- Cherry tomatoes, halved (optional)

Directions:

1. Cook the pasta according to package instructions until al dente. Drain and set aside.
2. In a food processor, combine the fresh basil leaves, grated Parmesan cheese, pine nuts, garlic cloves, and a pinch of salt and pepper. Pulse until well combined.
3. While the food processor is running, slowly drizzle in the olive oil until the mixture forms a smooth pesto sauce. In a large skillet, heat a drizzle of olive oil over medium heat. Add the cooked pasta and the pesto sauce. Toss until the pasta is well coated with the sauce.
4. If desired, add halved cherry tomatoes to the skillet and cook for an additional 1-2 minutes until slightly softened.
5. Serve the pesto pasta hot, garnished with fresh basil leaves.

Nutritional Information (per serving): Calories: 400 Protein: 10g Carbohydrates: 35g Fat: 25g Fiber: 2g Cholesterol: 10mg Sodium: 200mg Potassium: 200mg

Minestrone Soup

Yield: 2-6 servings | Prep time: 10 minutes | Cook time: 30 minutes

Ingredients:

- 1 tbsp olive oil
- 1 onion, diced
- 2 carrots, diced
- 2 celery stalks, diced
- 2 cloves garlic, minced
- 1 can (14 oz) diced tomatoes
- 4 cups vegetable broth
- 1 tsp dried basil
- Fresh basil leaves, for garnish
- 1 tsp dried oregano
- 1/2 cup small pasta
- 1 can (14 oz) kidney beans, drained and rinsed
- 1 cup diced zucchini
- Salt and pepper to taste
- Grated Parmesan cheese, for garnish

Directions:

1. Sauté onion, carrots, celery, and garlic in olive oil.
2. Add diced tomatoes, vegetable broth, basil, and oregano. Simmer for 10 minutes.
3. Add pasta, kidney beans, and zucchini. Cook for 10-12 minutes.
4. Season with salt and pepper.
5. Serve hot, garnished with Parmesan cheese and basil leaves.

Nutritional Information (per serving): Calories: 220 Protein: 8g Carbohydrates: 40g Fat: 3g Fiber: 8g Cholesterol: 0mg Sodium: 800mg Potassium: 700mg

Panzanella Salad

Yield: 2-6 servings | Prep time: 15 minutes | Cook time: 0 minutes

Ingredients:

- 4 cups stale bread, cubed
- 2 cups tomatoes, diced
- 1 cucumber, diced
- 1 red onion, thinly sliced
- Salt and pepper to taste
- 1/4 cup fresh basil leaves, torn
- 1/4 cup fresh parsley, chopped
- 3 tbsp extra virgin olive oil
- 2 tbsp red wine vinegar

Directions:

1. Combine bread, tomatoes, cucumber, red onion, basil, and parsley in a bowl.
2. Drizzle with olive oil and red wine vinegar. Season with salt and pepper.
3. Toss to combine and let sit for 10 minutes.
4. Serve at room temperature.

Nutritional Information (per serving): Calories: 250 Protein: 4g Carbohydrates: 36g Fat: 10g Fiber: 3g Cholesterol: 0mg Sodium: 350mg Potassium: 350mg

Spinach and Ricotta Cannelloni

Yield: 2-6 servings | Prep time: 30 minutes | Cook time: 40 minutes

Ingredients:

- 8 cannelloni tubes
- 2 cups fresh spinach, chopped
- 1 cup ricotta cheese
- 1/2 cup grated Parmesan cheese
- 1 egg
- Fresh basil leaves, for garnish

- 2 cloves garlic, minced
- 1 cup marinara sauce
- 1 cup shredded mozzarella cheese
- Salt and pepper to taste

Directions:

1. Cook cannelloni tubes according to package instructions. Set aside.
2. In a bowl, mix spinach, ricotta, Parmesan, egg, garlic, salt, and pepper.
3. Fill cannelloni tubes with the spinach-ricotta mixture.
4. Spread marinara sauce in a baking dish and place filled cannelloni on top.
5. Pour remaining marinara sauce over cannelloni and sprinkle with mozzarella.
6. Bake at 375°F (190°C) for 25 minutes covered, then 15 minutes uncovered until golden.
7. Let rest briefly and garnish with fresh basil leaves.

Nutritional Information (per serving): Calories: 350 Protein: 18g Carbohydrates: 32g Fat: 16g Fiber: 3g Cholesterol: 85mg Sodium: 550mg Potassium: 350mg

Stuffed Bell Peppers

Yield: 2-6 servings | Prep time: 15 minutes | Cook time: 40 minutes

Ingredients:

- 4 bell peppers
- 1 cup cooked rice
- 1/2 lb ground beef
- 1/2 onion, diced
- 1 clove garlic, minced
- Salt and pepper to taste

- 1 cup diced tomatoes
- 1/2 cup shredded cheese
- 1 tbsp olive oil
- 1 tsp Italian seasoning

Directions:

1. Preheat oven to 375°F (190°C). Cut tops off bell peppers, remove seeds and membranes.
2. Sauté onion and garlic in olive oil until translucent.
3. Cook ground beef until browned, then drain fat.
4. Add tomatoes, rice, Italian seasoning, salt, and pepper to skillet. Cook for 2-3 minutes.
5. Fill bell peppers with beef and rice mixture.
6. Place stuffed peppers in baking dish, cover with foil.
7. Bake for 25 minutes, remove foil and sprinkle with cheese.
8. Bake for 10-15 minutes until cheese melts.
9. Let cool briefly before serving.

Nutritional Information (per serving): Calories: 250 Protein: 15g Carbohydrates: 20g Fat: 12g Fiber: 4g Cholesterol: 35mg Sodium: 350mg Potassium: 500mg

Mushroom Risotto

Yield: 2-6 servings | Prep time: 10 minutes | Cook time: 30 minutes

Ingredients:

- 1 1/2 cups Arborio rice
- 4 cups vegetable or chicken broth
- 1 cup sliced mushrooms
- 1/2 onion, finely chopped
- 2 cloves garlic, minced
- Fresh parsley, for garnish

- 1/2 cup grated Parmesan cheese
- 2 tbsp butter
- 2 tbsp olive oil
- 1/2 cup dry white wine (optional)
- Salt and pepper to taste

Directions:

1. Sauté onion, garlic, and mushrooms in butter and olive oil.
2. Add Arborio rice and cook for a minute.
3. If using, pour in white wine and cook until absorbed.
4. Gradually add warm broth, stirring until absorbed.
5. Cook until rice is al dente and creamy, about 20-25 minutes.
6. Stir in Parmesan cheese, season with salt and pepper.
7. Let risotto rest briefly before serving.
8. Garnish with fresh parsley.

Nutritional Information (per serving): Calories: 300 Protein: 8g Carbohydrates: 50g Fat: 8g Fiber: 3g Cholesterol: 15mg Sodium: 800mg Potassium: 250mg

Vegetable Lasagna

Yield: 2-6 servings | Prep time: 20 minutes | Cook time: 40 minutes

Ingredients:

- 9 lasagna noodles
- 2 cups marinara sauce
- 2 cups mixed vegetables
- 1 cup spinach leaves
- Seasonings: dried basil, dried oregano, salt, and pepper

- 1 cup ricotta cheese
- 1 cup shredded mozzarella cheese
- 1/4 cup grated Parmesan cheese
- 2 cloves garlic, minced

Directions:

1. Cook lasagna noodles, then set aside.
2. Sauté mixed vegetables and garlic until tender, add spinach and season.
3. Mix ricotta, half of mozzarella, and Parmesan cheese.
4. Layer: sauce, noodles, vegetables, cheese mixture. Repeat.
5. Top with remaining sauce, mozzarella, and Parmesan.
6. Bake covered at 375°F for 30 minutes.
7. Uncover and bake for 10 more minutes until golden.
8. Rest before serving.

Nutritional Information (per serving): Calories: 350 Protein: 18g Carbs: 45g Fat: 11g Fiber: 6g Cholesterol: 35mg Sodium: 700mg Potassium: 500mg

Pasta Aglio e Olio (Garlic and Oil Pasta)

Yield: 2-6 servings | Prep time: 5 minutes | Cook time: 15 minutes

Ingredients:

- 8 ounces spaghetti
- 1/3 cup extra-virgin olive oil
- 4 cloves garlic, thinly sliced
- 1/2 teaspoon red pepper flakes
- Grated Parmesan cheese (optional)
- Salt, to taste
- Freshly ground black pepper, to taste
- 1/4 cup chopped fresh parsley

Directions:

1. Cook spaghetti according to package instructions until al dente. Drain and set aside.
2. Heat olive oil in a large skillet over medium heat. Add garlic and red pepper flakes. Cook until garlic turns golden brown and fragrant.
3. Add cooked spaghetti to the skillet. Toss well to coat the pasta with the garlic-infused oil. Season with salt and black pepper.
4. Remove from heat and sprinkle with chopped parsley. Toss again to combine.
5. Serve hot, optionally garnished with grated Parmesan cheese.

Nutritional Information (per serving): Calories: 350 Protein: 8g Carbohydrates: 45g Fat: 16g Fiber: 2g Cholesterol: 0mg Sodium: 200mg Potassium: 150mg

Desserts

Tiramisu

Yield: 4 servings | Prep time: 30 min | Cook time: 20 min

Ingredients:

- 6 egg yolks
- 3/4 cup sugar
- 2/3 cup milk
- 1 1/4 cups heavy cream
- 24 ladyfingers
- 2 tbsp unsweetened cocoa powder
- 1/2 tsp vanilla extract
- 8 oz mascarpone cheese
- 1 cup strong brewed coffee, cooled

Directions:

1. Whisk yolks and sugar until creamy.
2. Heat milk, add to yolks, and cook until thickened. Let yolk mixture cool.
3. Beat cream and vanilla until stiff, fold in mascarpone.
4. Dip ladyfingers in coffee and layer in dish.
5. Spread half of mascarpone mixture over ladyfingers.
6. Repeat with another layer.
7. Sift cocoa powder on top.
8. Refrigerate for 4 hours or overnight.

Nutritional Information (per serving): Calories: 356 Protein: 8g Carbs: 34g Fat: 20g Fiber: 1g Cholesterol: 243mg Sodium: 51mg Potassium: 140mg.

Cannoli

Yield: 4 servings | Prep time: 20 minutes | Cook time: 10 minutes

Ingredients:

- 8 cannoli shells
- 1 1/2 cups ricotta cheese
- 1/2 cup powdered sugar
- Powdered sugar, for dusting
- 1/4 teaspoon vanilla extract
- 1/4 cup chopped pistachios
- 1/4 cup mini chocolate chips

Directions:

1. In a medium bowl, combine the ricotta cheese, powdered sugar, and vanilla extract. Mix until smooth and well combined.
2. Fill a piping bag fitted with a large round tip with the ricotta mixture.
3. Gently pipe the ricotta filling into each end of the cannoli shells, filling them completely.
4. Dip the ends of the filled cannoli shells into the chopped pistachios and mini chocolate chips, allowing them to adhere to the ricotta filling.
5. Dust the cannoli with powdered sugar just before serving.
6. Serve immediately or refrigerate for up to 2 hours before serving to allow the flavors to meld.

Nutritional Information: (per serving) Calories: 275 Protein: 10g Carbohydrates: 28g Fat: 14g Fiber: 1g Cholesterol: 28mg Sodium: 88mg Potassium: 130mg.

Gelato

Yield: 4 servings | Prep time: 15 min | Cook time: 30 min

Ingredients:

- 2 cups whole milk
- 1 cup heavy cream
- 3/4 cup sugar
- Flavorings of choice (e.g., chocolate chips, fruit puree, nuts)
- 4 large egg yolks
- 1 tsp vanilla extract
- Pinch of salt

Directions:

1. Heat milk and cream in a saucepan until simmering.
2. Whisk sugar, egg yolks, vanilla, and salt in a separate bowl.
3. Slowly pour hot milk mixture into the egg yolk mixture, whisking constantly.
4. Cook combined mixture over low heat until thickened.
5. Let it cool, then refrigerate for at least 4 hours.
6. Churn in an ice cream maker, adding flavorings during the last few minutes.
7. Freeze for 2-4 hours to firm up.
8. Serve and enjoy!

Nutritional Information: (per serving) Calories: 320 Protein: 6g Carbs: 32g Fat: 19g Fiber: 0g Cholesterol: 200mg Sodium: 60mg Potassium: 220mg.

Panna Cotta

Yield: 4 servings | Prep time: 10 min | Cook time: 10 min

Ingredients:

- 2 cups heavy cream
- 1/2 cup milk
- 1/2 cup sugar
- 2 tbsp cold water
- 2 tsp vanilla extract
- 2 1/2 tsp gelatin powder

Directions:

1. Heat cream, milk, and sugar in a saucepan until hot.
2. Remove from heat, add vanilla extract.
3. Bloom gelatin in cold water, then add to the cream mixture.
4. Stir until gelatin dissolves.
5. Pour into serving glasses and refrigerate for 4 hours or until set.
6. Serve plain or with desired toppings.

Nutritional Information: (per serving) Calories: 380 Protein: 4g Carbs: 27g Fat: 29g Fiber: 0g Cholesterol: 90mg Sodium: 50mg Potassium: 150mg.

Zabaione

Yield: 4 servings | Prep time: 5 minutes | Cook time: 10 minutes

Ingredients:

- 4 large egg yolks
- 1/4 cup granulated sugar
- 1/4 cup sweet Marsala wine
- 1/2 teaspoon vanilla extract

Directions:

1. In a heatproof bowl, whisk together the egg yolks and sugar until well combined and creamy.
2. Place the bowl over a pot of simmering water, making sure the bottom of the bowl doesn't touch the water.
3. Gradually whisk in the Marsala wine and continue whisking constantly for about 8-10 minutes, or until the mixture thickens and doubles in volume. It should have a smooth and creamy consistency.
4. Remove the bowl from the heat and whisk in the vanilla extract.
5. Serve the zabaione immediately while it's still warm, either on its own or as a topping for desserts like fresh fruit, cake, or ice cream.

Nutritional Information: (per serving) Calories: 180 Protein: 5g Carbohydrates: 19g Fat: 8g Fiber: 0g Cholesterol: 425mg Sodium: 15mg Potassium: 90mg.

Panettone

Yield: 1 large panettone | Prep time: 20 min | Cook time: 45-55 min

Ingredients:

- 4 cups all-purpose flour
- 1/2 cup sugar
- 1 tbsp active dry yeast
- 1/2 cup warm water
- 1/2 cup softened butter
- 4 large eggs
- 1/2 cup raisins
- 1/2 cup candied citrus peel
- 1/4 tsp salt
- 1 tsp vanilla extract
- Zest of 1 lemon
- Zest of 1 orange

Directions:

1. Dissolve yeast in warm water and let it sit for 5 min.
2. Combine flour, sugar, salt, yeast mixture, butter, eggs, vanilla extract, lemon zest, and orange zest in a bowl.
3. Knead the dough for 10 min until smooth.
4. Let the dough rise for 1-2 hours.
5. Knead in raisins and candied citrus peel.
6. Shape the dough and let it rise for another 1-2 hours.
7. Bake at 350°F (175°C) for 45-55 min.
8. Cool before serving.

Nutritional Information: (per serving) Calories: 315 Protein: 7g Carbs: 54g Fat: 8g Fiber: 2g Cholesterol: 69mg Sodium: 75mg Potassium: 192mg.

Biscotti

Yield: 24 biscotti | Prep time: 15 min | Cook time: 40 min

Ingredients:

- 2 cups all-purpose flour
- 1 cup sugar
- 1 tsp baking powder
- 1/4 tsp salt
- 1/2 cup dried cranberries or chocolate chips (optional)
- 3 large eggs
- 1 tsp vanilla extract
- 1 cup chopped nuts

Directions:

1. Mix flour, sugar, baking powder, and salt in a bowl.
2. Beat eggs and vanilla extract in a separate bowl.
3. Combine wet and dry ingredients to form a dough.
4. Stir in nuts and optional cranberries or chocolate chips.
5. Shape dough into logs and bake at 350°F (175°C) for 25-30 min.
6. Cool logs for 10 min, then slice into biscotti.
7. Bake sliced biscotti for an additional 10 min until crisp.
8. Let biscotti cool completely before serving.

Nutrition information: (per serving) Calories: 120 Protein: 3g Carbs: 20g Fat: 3g Fiber: 1g Cholesterol: 30mg Sodium: 60mg Potassium: 60mg.

Zeppole

Yield: 4 servings | Prep time: 15 min | Cook time: 15 min

Ingredients:

- 1 cup water
- 1/2 cup unsalted butter
- 1 tbsp sugar
- 1/4 tsp salt
- Vegetable oil, for frying
- 1 cup all-purpose flour
- 4 large eggs
- Powdered sugar, for dusting

Directions:

1. Boil water, butter, sugar, and salt in a saucepan.
2. Add flour and stir until dough forms.
3. Let the dough cool slightly.
4. Beat in eggs, one at a time, until smooth.
5. Heat oil to 350°F (175°C) in a pot.
6. Drop spoonfuls of dough into the hot oil and fry until golden brown.
7. Remove zeppole and drain on paper towels.
8. Dust with powdered sugar and serve warm.

Nutrition information: (per serving) Calories: 250 Protein: 6g Carbs: 22g Fat: 16g Fiber: 1g Cholesterol: 150mg Sodium: 100mg Potassium: 80mg.

Torta della Nonna

Yield: 6 servings | Prep time: 30 min | Cook time: 45 min

Ingredients:

- Puff pastry sheet
- 2 cups milk
- 4 egg yolks
- 1/2 cup sugar
- Powdered sugar, for dusting
- 1/4 cup flour
- 1/2 tsp vanilla extract
- Zest of 1 lemon

Directions:

1. Line cake pan with puff pastry.
2. Simmer milk in a saucepan.
3. Whisk egg yolks, sugar, flour, vanilla, and lemon zest.
4. Gradually add hot milk to the egg mixture.
5. Cook custard on low heat until thickened.
6. Pour custard over puff pastry and bake at 350°F (175°C) for 40-45 min.
7. Cool to room temperature and dust with powdered sugar.

Nutrition information: (per serving) Calories: 320 Protein: 7g Carbs: 42g Fat: 14g Fiber: 1g Cholesterol: 150mg Sodium: 100mg Potassium: 180mg.

Sfogliatelle

Yield: 12 servings | Prep time: 60 min | Cook time: 25 min

Ingredients:

- 2 cups all-purpose flour
- 1/4 cup sugar
- 1/4 tsp salt
- 1/2 cup chilled butter, diced
- 1/2 cup water
- 1 cup semolina
- 1/4 cup chopped almonds (optional)
- 1 cup ricotta cheese
- 1/2 cup powdered sugar
- 1/2 tsp vanilla extract
- Zest of 1 lemon
- 1/4 cup candied orange peel (optional)

Directions:

1. Mix flour, sugar, and salt. Cut in chilled butter.
2. Gradually add water and knead the dough.
3. Rest the dough in the refrigerator for 30 min.
4. Cook semolina with water until thickened.
5. Combine ricotta, powdered sugar, vanilla, lemon zest, orange peel, and almonds.
6. Roll out dough, spread semolina mixture, and roll tightly.
7. Cut into slices and bake at 375°F (190°C) for 25 min.
8. Cool slightly and dust with powdered sugar.

Nutrition information: (per serving) Calories: 270 Protein: 6g Carbs: 32g Fat: 13g Fiber: 1g Cholesterol: 35mg Sodium: 80mg Potassium: 120mg.

Amaretti

Yield: 24 servings | Prep time: 15 min | Cook time: 15 min

Ingredients:

- 2 cups almond flour
- 1 cup sugar
- Powdered sugar, for dusting
- 2 egg whites
- 1/2 tsp almond extract

Directions:

1. Combine almond flour and sugar.
2. Whisk egg whites until frothy.
3. Add egg whites and almond extract to the flour mixture. Mix into a dough.
4. Roll into small balls and flatten.
5. Bake at 325°F (165°C) for 15 min until golden.
6. Cool on a wire rack.
7. Dust with powdered sugar.

Nutrition information: (per serving) Calories: 60 Protein: 1g Carbs: 7g Fat: 3g Fiber: 1g Cholesterol: 0mg Sodium: 5mg Potassium: 20mg.

Torte Caprese

Yield: 8 servings | Prep time: 15 min | Cook time: 40 min

Ingredients:

- 200g dark chocolate
- 200g butter
- 200g sugar
- Powdered sugar, for dusting
- 4 eggs
- 150g almond flour
- 1 tsp vanilla extract

Directions:

1. Melt chocolate and butter together.
2. Whisk eggs and sugar until fluffy.
3. Gradually add chocolate mixture to the eggs, whisking.
4. Fold in almond flour and vanilla extract.
5. Pour batter into greased cake pan.
6. Bake at 350°F (180°C) for 35-40 min.
7. Cool in pan for 10 min, then transfer to wire rack.
8. Dust with powdered sugar.

Nutrition information: (per serving) Calories: 380 Protein: 7g Carbs: 28g Fat: 28g Fiber: 4g Cholesterol: 95mg Sodium: 65mg Potassium: 230mg.

Cassata Siciliana

Yield: 8 servings | Prep time: 30 min | Cook time: 0 min

Ingredients:

- 500g ricotta cheese
- 150g powdered sugar
- 100g candied fruit
- 50g grated dark chocolate
- Powdered sugar, for dusting
- 2 tbsp orange liqueur
- 8 slices of sponge cake
- 200g marzipan
- Green food coloring

Directions:

1. Mix ricotta, powdered sugar, candied fruit, chocolate, and liqueur.
2. Line a cake pan with plastic wrap and layer with sponge cake.
3. Spread ricotta mixture and add another layer of cake.
4. Chill for 2 hours.
5. Color marzipan green and shape into decorations.
6. Unmold the cassata and decorate with marzipan.
7. Dust with powdered sugar.

Nutrition information: (per serving) Calories: 370 Protein: 10g Carbs: 45g Fat: 16g Fiber: 2g Cholesterol: 35mg Sodium: 150mg Potassium: 200mg.

Struffoli

Yield: 6 servings | Prep time: 30 min | Cook time: 15 min

Ingredients:

- 2 cups all-purpose flour
- 3 large eggs
- 2 tbsp sugar
- 1 tbsp butter, melted
- Candied fruit or sprinkles, for decoration
- 1/2 tsp vanilla extract
- Vegetable oil, for frying
- Honey, for coating

Directions:

1. Mix flour, eggs, sugar, melted butter, vanilla, and salt to form a dough.
2. Knead the dough and cut into small pieces.
3. Fry in oil until golden brown, then coat with warm honey.
4. Shape into a mound and decorate with candied fruit.

Nutrition information: (per serving) Calories: 320 Protein: 5g Carbs: 55g Fat: 9g Fiber: 1g Cholesterol: 70mg Sodium: 60mg Potassium: 60mg.

Pizzelle

Yield: 24 servings | Prep time: 10 minutes | Cook time: 20 minutes

Ingredients:

- 2 cups all-purpose flour
- 1 cup granulated sugar
- 1/2 cup unsalted butter, melted
- Powdered sugar, for dusting
- 3 large eggs
- 1 tsp vanilla extract
- 1/2 tsp baking powder

Directions:

- In a mixing bowl, beat the eggs and sugar until well combined.
- Add the melted butter and vanilla extract, and mix until smooth.
- In a separate bowl, whisk together the flour and baking powder.
- Gradually add the dry ingredients to the wet ingredients, mixing until a smooth batter forms.
- Preheat a pizzelle iron and lightly grease with cooking spray.
- Drop spoonfuls of batter onto the iron and close it, cooking for about 1 minute or until golden brown.
- Carefully remove the pizzelle from the iron and let them cool on a wire rack.
- Repeat with the remaining batter.
- Once cooled, dust the pizzelle with powdered sugar before serving.

Nutritional Information: (per serving) Calories: 120 Protein: 2g Carbohydrates: 18g Fat: 5g Fiber: 0g Cholesterol: 35mg Sodium: 10mg Potassium: 20mg.